Don't Tell
Anybody
the Secrets
I Told You

Don't Tell Anybody the Secrets I Told You

A Memoir

Lucinda Williams

**SIMON &
SCHUSTER**

London · New York · Sydney · Toronto · New Delhi

First published in the United States by Crown, an imprint of Random House, a division of Penguin Random House LLC, New York, 2023

First published in Great Britain by Simon & Schuster UK Ltd, 2023

1 3 5 7 9 10 8 6 4 2

Simon & Schuster UK Ltd
1st Floor
222 Gray's Inn Road
London WC1X 8HB

www.simonandschuster.co.uk
www.simonandschuster.com.au
www.simonandschuster.co.in

Simon & Schuster Australia, Sydney
Simon & Schuster India, New Delhi

A CIP catalogue record for this book
is available from the British Library

Hardback ISBN: 978-1-4711-7748-4
eBook ISBN: 978-1-4711-7750-7

Printed and Bound in the UK using 100% Renewable Electricity at CPI Group (UK) Ltd

My life has been a labor of love,
as has this book,
which I dedicate to my father,
Miller Williams,
and his parents,
Rev. Ernest Burdette and
Ann Jeanette Miller Williams.
They understood and taught me
the power of language and music
to create a more just world.

CHRONOLOGY OF PLACES WHERE I LIVED

1953	Born. Lake Charles, Louisiana
1954	Iowa; Louisiana
1955	Vicksburg, Mississippi
1955	Utah
1957	Jackson, Mississippi
1958	Macon, Georgia
1963	Baton Rouge, Louisiana
1964	Santiago, Chile
1965	Baton Rouge, Louisiana
1966	New Orleans
1970	Mexico City
1971	Fayetteville, Arkansas
1972	New Orleans
1973	Fayetteville, Arkansas
1974	San Francisco
1974	Fayetteville, Arkansas
1974–1979	Houston and Austin, Texas
1979	New York City
1980–1984	Houston and Austin, Texas
1984–1991	Los Angeles
1991	Nashville
2000s	Los Angeles
2020s	Nashville

INTERVIEWER: When someone finds this book fifty years from now, what do you want them to find in it?

LUCINDA: I want them to see, to really see, to get underneath the covers and see how things really were and not have it be sugarcoated. I don't want it to be one of those sugarcoated books like you find at Walgreens. I want them to see the truth. And I would hope that it would help people who maybe had some mental illness in their family. I would hope they can read about what was going on in my family and be able to connect with it.

Don't Tell
Anybody
the Secrets
I Told You

1

In the summer my father would drink gin and tonics. When I was a kid, he would say, "Honey, can you go make me a drink?" I knew how to pour gin into a shot glass and into the cocktail glass with ice and then pour in the tonic, add a piece of lime. Nobody back then thought there was anything bad about that. I remember reading an article about Eudora Welty describing how she would have one small glass of whiskey in the late afternoons before dinner. It was her little treat, a way of relaxing at the end of the day, having a cocktail. In the same manner, my dad and my stepmother, Jordan, who I called Momma Jordan or Momma J, would partake of a glass of wine or a cocktail at the end of the day, and my dad would open the day's mail and we'd talk about current events or anything else. We'd sit in the sunroom off the living room. It was all glass and it felt like you were sitting outside. You could enjoy that room all year round because you didn't have to worry about bugs but you could enjoy the natural light. In the winter it would be delightful because there was a potbelly heater out there to warm the room.

I had different experiences with my mother and her drinking. She was not a social drinker. She drank in private, a closet drinker. I didn't realize this until I was around age eighteen when I was visiting my mother at her apartment in New Orleans and she came to the door slurring her words. For years she had always said it was her medications. I was used to seeing her like that. She had spent a lot of time in mental health hospitals and various therapy clinics and she was on medications. But it suddenly occurred to me on this visit with her in New Orleans that on top of that she was drinking heavily. I didn't know she was an alcoholic until then.

Her maternal instincts or maternal abilities were taken from her by her mental illness. We were close until she passed away in 2004, but after a certain point I didn't depend on her for anything. I learned at a very early age that I wouldn't be getting from my mother what most kids get from their mothers, the stability and warmth and reliability and support. I never felt any pressure from her, either. I mean, she didn't have that capacity.

Looking back on it, many of my traits that might be considered good traits came from her. She read everything. She played piano and she listened to good music. She loved Judy

Garland and Erroll Garner and Ray Charles. She also introduced me to Joan Baez and Leonard Cohen. As I grew older and more aware of her mental illness, I began to compare her situation to that of Sylvia Plath and in many ways to Anne Sexton. Both Plath and Sexton committed suicide. My mother didn't commit suicide, but she did check out in other ways, at least from the point of view of her children.

My mother was obsessed with psychotherapy and read every book about it that she could get her hands on. She was in therapy all the time and in and out of psychiatric hospitals. She had electroshock treatment back when they didn't have the drugs for depression that we have now. She was on lithium and she hated it. Lithium had horrible side effects, like nausea and diarrhea and skin problems and weight gain and fatigue. Because of that she'd stop taking the pills. Then she would act out in a very hostile manner and my father would say, "Oh, she's not taking her medication." That's a lot for a kid to deal with. Early in my life everything involving my mother revolved around hospitals and therapists and drugs.

I was always hearing comments from my father like "Your mother's not well, it's not her fault, your mother's not well, don't be mad at your mother." I understood that. It was actually a sort of generous thing for him to say about her. But I was left without very much to grasp on to. I would think, "Okay, my mother isn't here for me." I understood that. It wasn't easy. I had to pick my spots and pick my times when it was okay to engage her.

My mother's name was Lucille Fern Day and she was born on December 31, 1930. Her parents were the Reverend Ernest Wyman Day and Alva Bernice Coon Day. She went by Lucy. Her father was a Methodist minister, so conservative you'd think he might have been Baptist. He was a hellfire-and-brimstone type of evangelical preacher. The Methodist Church moved him from town to town in Louisiana every two or three years. Both of my grandfathers were Methodist ministers, but my mother's family was much more closed-minded. She had four brothers, three older and one younger. Her younger brother, Robert, died on his motorcycle coming home from World War II. That was before I was born. I always heard from my mother that he was the sensitive one in the family. He was a poet and, along with my mother, a musician. My little brother, Robert, was named after him.

Mom studied music but didn't pursue a career in it. My understanding is that she started playing piano at the age of four. She fell in love with it. But music became her albatross, the piano was her albatross, because she wasn't allowed or able to pursue it as a career. It became a symbol for what she could not do. Nobody in her family encouraged her to take it seriously. I'm not going to say that her inability to pursue a career in music caused her mental illness, or influenced it, because I think most of it was biochemical. But she struggled so much with not having a career in music. It affected her confidence or lack thereof.

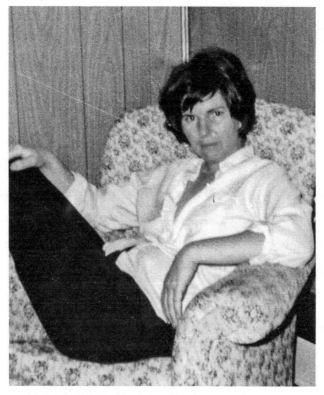

My mother, Lucille Fern Day.

We had a piano in the house when I was growing up. After my parents divorced, Mama still had a piano with her wherever she lived. But the piano would come and go. It was a joy and a burden at the same time, a love-hate relationship. She would long for a piano and then get rid of it after a while. She never explained why and I didn't ask. When those feelings overwhelmed her, she would get rid of the piano. Then a short time later she'd go out and get another one. It was back and forth; she couldn't live with a piano or without a piano. She wasn't like Bette Davis in one of those old movies, running around with smeared lipstick. Her mental illness was more understated and subtle and at the same time monumental.

My mother told me that when she was a kid, her family didn't have plumbing and they used newspapers for wallpaper and insulation. They were all working-class and didn't care about school or going to college. I don't know how one sibling can be born into the same family as other siblings, and grow up the same way, and come out so different. She had an intellectual mind, read good books. It was a testament to her capabilities that she broke out and went to college and became a well-read person because none of her relatives were like that at all.

My mother met my father when she was studying music at LSU. My mother's family hated my father. He was the literary poet guy. Although they were both church families, his family was liberal and open-minded. My mother wanted to be in a more progressive world and my father offered a way into it.

Later in my life my father told me certain things about my mother being sexually molested in horrifying ways by her father and one or more of her older brothers, repeatedly, when she was a youth. This was confirmed to me later by my sister, Karyn, who attended therapy sessions with my mother when she was older. Karyn didn't tell me this for years and years and I don't think she made the wrong decision to withhold it. Learning about this was unthinkably horrifying and upsetting, and I'm still trying to process it.

I have memories of my mother being happy, and of us being happy together. She had a great sense of humor. We would laugh at all sorts of things. But she would drift in and out of her illness like Sylvia Plath did. My father told me that she was once diagnosed as having manic depression with paranoid schizophrenic tendencies. Back then they didn't have the medication we have now.

Mom talked about her psychiatric care and would quote passages from her psychology books and jot notes in the margins. She read Jung and she read that popular book from the 1960s *I'm OK—You're OK*. She was very aware of her mental illness. After I moved away, we would talk on the phone for hours about psychology and the latest therapies. I learned so much from her.

She was sent into mental hospitals from time to time after she had nervous breakdowns. My father used to say that everything with her seemed fine when they were dating and before they got married. Then they got married and they didn't have much money. My father was a struggling itinerant professor moving around and working at various colleges. This was in the early 1950s and my mother wasn't working, because most women did all their work at home.

I was born on January 26, 1953, in Lake Charles, Louisiana. You could say that I was a born fighter. Like most people I don't have a clear memory of my earliest years, but my father always told me that right from the beginning I had to fight. I was born with spina bifida, which is obviously not the best malady for someone who would go on to spend a couple of hours every night standing on a stage, but I've managed to overcome that just fine. As a young child I was often sick. When I was about one year old, my windpipe became blocked and I had an emergency tracheotomy. My father said it was touch and go, but I made it. I still have a visible scar from that procedure, and every time I look in a mirror, it's a reminder of my difficult beginning and that it's possible to grow stronger. My struggles continued for another couple of years. At one point I developed croup and had to be put in the hospital in one of those oxygen humidity tents, and then I was quarantined at home in another oxygen tent in my bedroom.

Things grew more difficult between my parents after I was born, and my father always said I got the worst of it. I was their first baby and the responsibilities caused all sorts of new stresses and new tensions. When I was very young, my mother would get in these hostile moods and nobody ever knew what caused it or triggered it. My brother, Robert, was born two years later and my sister, Karyn, two years after him.

For years, as both a teenager and an adult, whenever I was having my own problems, my dad would say to me, "Well, honey, once when you were three years old, before your brother and sister were born, I came home from work and your mother had locked you in a closet because you were being a typical three-year-old and crying and she couldn't handle it." That was his explanation for my troubles. He was intellectually minded and was really into Freud. So he was always analyzing things, and he would tell me that story as an explanation of how things were for me as a child. Mom wasn't being mean, he'd say. She just couldn't deal with it. She probably thought I was safer locked in the closet. When I think about it now, it sounds so horrible. How could a mother do that? But there was always my dad there to say, "She can't help it. It's not her fault. She's not well."

My mother used to tell me stories about how poor we were when I was a baby and toddler. She said she had to borrow bread from the neighbors to feed us. Also, they didn't have a crib for me, so she pulled a drawer from a chest and turned that into my bed. Poverty put even more stress on my parents' already fragile relationship.

If a child drops something on the floor, a healthy family would say, "Oh, that's okay, honey, we'll clean it up." My mother would say, "Goddamn it!" Everybody was walking on eggshells around her. My dad wasn't Mr. Perfect, either. He would get irritable and I never knew what kind of mood he was going to be in. Sometimes he would say things to me like "If you keep doing that, I'm going to knock your teeth down your throat."

But I bonded with my father in a way that I might not have if my mother had been more stable, if she'd been more available to me emotionally. When my mother would be really bad off—yelling, screaming, cussing, throwing things at my dad or at the wall—he would take us out to play Putt-Putt or to see a drive-in movie, anything to get us out of the house. He took on the role of what a mother would do back in those times. Despite this, I didn't grow up hating her, or feeling any kind of resentment, because of my dad always saying, "It's not her fault. She's not well."

My father and me.

Recently my sister, Karyn, and I were looking at some old family pictures and out of the blue she brought up a memory of us playing Putt-Putt. I could not believe it. She's four years younger than me, but she had the exact same memories of playing Putt-Putt with my father. That was a very powerful moment for me.

I'm seventy years old and I'm still working through a lot of this. I've held back from talking about my childhood over the decades of my life—I've written songs about it instead—because I think I came to think of it as normal. "Okay, my mother is freaking out and yelling; my dad is in a bad mood today." I could tell that everybody was trying. And that seemed normal, the trying.

I still remember one of my favorite photographs of my father and me. I'm about two years old. We're standing on the front steps of our house, and it looks like we were getting ready to go to church, or we had just come back from church, because he's got his suit on, and I have a little dress and a little jacket on. It just has such a sweetness and innocence to it. The two of us are just on the front steps together. You can see we had this special bond. I had been so sick, and by the time I was born, my mother's mental illness had started to rear its ugly head, so my father was taking care of me more and more.

Now that I've read a lot of psychology books and been through extensive therapy and self-education on mental illness and dysfunctional families, I realize that I didn't have any way to recognize or deal with this trauma that happened to me. Kids will end up blaming themselves. All of that energy goes somewhere. You're the little kid sitting in

With my dad in front of our house.

the locked closet, thinking and feeling, "What did I do that was wrong?" But then my dad was saying, "It's not her fault, she's not well, you can't be angry at your mother." What was I going to do with all that sadness and confusion and anger?

Not long after we moved to Baton Rouge, when I was eight years old, I was sent to see a child therapist. I vaguely remember just sitting in a room with this woman, playing some kind of board game. My dad told me something like "Well, we were concerned that maybe you were, you know . . . because of your mother's illness." I don't think I was acting out or anything. It was just a matter of precaution. "We need to make sure everything's good," he said. Maybe my mother was going through a particularly bad time and he feared I was being traumatized by it.

A couple of years ago, I was in a bar in New York and an older gentleman came up to me and asked me what I was working on. I said this book. He'd had something to do with the music business. He told me, "Don't write about your childhood. Nobody wants to read about that. Just write about your music. Just pick a part of your career to write about." But my childhood informs so many of my songs. Some listeners hear these memories and feelings in my songs. One woman came up to me after a show at the Dakota in Minneapolis and asked, "Did you have a rough childhood?" I nodded my head as I was making my way backstage. "I thought so," she said.

I can remember going to my uncle and aunt's house in Baton Rouge to spend the night with my cousins. It was more like my parents dumping us off to get rid of us for a day or two. This was my mother's brother and his wife and their twin daughters, two girls who constantly fought each other. Their mother, my aunt, was a very religious woman with jet-black dyed hair. She would put food coloring in pancake batter and make the pancakes all kinds of different colors.

My mother's mother, my grandmother, would pull switches from the hickory tree in their yard and whip us with them when she thought we'd done something bad. I can't imagine how my mother felt growing up in that family, undergoing the abusive trauma that she experienced and also just living among people who didn't follow the news or even know who was mayor or governor or anything. There are those of us for whom this is real life.

Forty years later I wrote the song "Bus to Baton Rouge," which came out on my album *Essence,* in 2001. Some people have told me they think it's one of my most beautiful songs, almost a gospel hymn. It's definitely one of my most documentary songs. It's about my mother's family and her parents' house in Baton Rouge that we visited all the time. The verses of the song go like this:

> I had to go back to that house one more time
> To see if the camellias were in bloom.
> For so many reasons it's been on my mind
> The house on Belmont Avenue.
>
> Built up on cinder blocks off of the ground
> What with the rain and the soft swampy land.
> By the sweet honeysuckle that grew all around
> Were switches when we were bad.
>
> I took a bus to Baton Rouge . . .

All the front rooms were kept closed off
I never liked to go in there much.
Sometimes the doors they'd be locked
'Cause there were precious things that I couldn't
  touch.

... The company couch covered in plastic
Little books about being saved.
The dining room table that nobody ate at
And the piano that nobody played.

I took a bus to Baton Rouge ...

There was a beautiful lamp I always loved
A seashore was painted on the shade.
It would turn around when you switched on the
  bulb
And gently rock the waves.

... The driveway was covered with tiny white
  seashells
A fig tree stood in the backyard.
There are other things I remember as well,
But to tell them would just be too hard.

Ghosts in the wind that blow through my life
Follow me wherever I go.
I'll never be free from these chains inside
Hidden deep down in my soul.

I took a bus to Baton Rouge ...

The "ghosts in the wind that blow through my life"— many of them I didn't even know about until much later, but they followed me nonetheless.

My dad used to say that we carry our roots forward, so for me to tell my story and where my foundation comes from really has to begin with my roots—my family and the people whose sensibilities and ideals I inherited. Even though my mother's family was so different, it's easy for me to find myself in my ancestry. Both of my grandfathers, paternal and maternal, were Methodist preachers, one in Louisiana, the other in Arkansas. Being a Methodist preacher meant that you had to move from church to church, community to community. So that's the life both my mother and my father knew from growing up. Then, once they were married, my mother and father also moved our family from place to place in search of new work. Although I was born in Lake Charles, Louisiana, we didn't live there long. My brother was born in Vicksburg, Mississippi, when I was two, and my sister was born in Jackson when I was four. I know that we also lived in Utah for a year, because my mother used to say, "Honey, don't forget to tell people that we lived in Utah," and there's a picture of the car, this 1950-something Chevy or Ford, in the snow. Those were pretty rough years. But I didn't grow up feeling poor. Nobody ever used that word. Financially we struggled, but it was considered just part of life, to get from point A to point B or point whatever.

My father was first a scientist and then a poet—not your typical career trajectory—and always scrambling around for teaching jobs. He didn't get a permanent teaching job until I was eighteen years old. By then we had lived in twelve different towns since I was born. I can remember nine of them. They say moving is one of the most stressful things that happens in life. Well, I moved twelve times before I was eighteen.

I've always been comfortable on the road, moving around to keep my career going. It's in my blood. I feel at home on buses and in hotels and then standing in front of people, almost like a traveling preacher, and expressing what I believe the most, what I care about the most, which is my music. And much of my music is about my life, so it's like a story that keeps being lived and told, written and sung.

The souls of my paternal grandfather and grandmother, Ernest Burdette Williams and Ann Jeanette Miller Williams, found their way into my life through my father. In contrast to my mother's parents, his parents were impressive people. By the time my grandfather became a Methodist minister in Hoxie, Arkansas, he had already been a teacher, a county tax assessor, a cashier at a bank, and a club baseball pitcher. My father, Stanley Miller Williams, was born in Hoxie in 1930. He was the fourth child of what would become six children. When he was born, my grandparents had already lost five children, including two in the great flu epidemic of 1918.

Ernest was a progressive minister, a social democrat. At every new church he insisted that anyone be allowed to sit in the congregation regardless of race, which was controversial because it stood against the segregation laws at the time. My grandparents were once held at gunpoint in Fort Smith, Arkansas, by a man who said he needed to teach them "southern manners." Apparently, my grandmother had been seen speaking with black people as she rode on one of the town's streetcars and the white folks in that town weren't supposed to do that.

Not long after my father was born, my grandfather invited Harry Leland Mitchell to hold secret meetings in the basement of his church. Mitchell was a socialist and a sharecropper who was fighting for better conditions from the landowners for sharecroppers. This was the beginning of what became the Southern Tenant Farmers' Union, which Mitchell founded in 1934 to help sharecroppers and tenant farmers get better deals during the Great Depression. It was one of the few unions in America in the 1930s that was open to both white and black people.

Ernest also stood with other ministers against Arkansas's governor, Orval Faubus, in the public school conflict in 1957, when nine black students were prevented from enrolling in Little Rock Central High School. Faubus used the Arkansas National Guard to stop these kids from entering the school. There was a Presbyterian minister named Dunbar Ogden who led an effort to bring together ministers who supported integration. Many of those ministers, including my grandfather, risked losing their congregations because of their support for integration.

All these stories were a big part of the family lore on my father's side—told and retold—and that's where my father got his progressive streak and probably where I got mine. As a kid I would go to hear my grandfather preach and afterward I would talk with my father about it. I was too young to really understand what was going on, but something about what I heard stuck with me. My father told me how his father was preaching about equal rights for women and against Jim Crow laws of segregation. He also argued against censorship in the arts and the news.

A few years ago in my father's belongings I found a book of my grandfather's printed sermons that my father had put together. Reading those sermons blew my mind. Here's a paragraph from one from the late 1940s, but it might as well be from the 2020s:

In all the areas of human life there is a fierce struggle for control going on between those who want to restore a vanished past and those who want to create a better future. There are those who want to set the world back in the precise order it was before the two World Wars and the world wide Depression, as one would arrange a living room after a wild party the night before. There are the profiteers who want to get all four feet back in the financial trough in which they used to wallow. There are the lip servants of democracy who are willing to use the world as a fighting slogan, but have no use for democracy when it means giving equal opportunities to all peoples, or when it means lifting millions all about us to where the four freedoms would apply to them, too.

In July 2022 when I was in Vancouver touring with Bonnie Raitt, my tour manager came up to me one night and said there was an elderly man who would like to chat with me. The man was Don Todd, a retired philosophy professor at Simon Fraser University. He was almost ninety-two years old. He was dressed very much the way my father would have dressed—tan slacks and a button-down shirt, a professor's look.

He'd known my dad growing up and told me stories about him and my grandfather. He told me that my grandfather was from a very small town, just a village, way back in the rural mountains in the northern part of Arkansas. There were no roads there, no cars, just mountain trails. There was a tiny little school there that had one teacher for six grades. The school ended at sixth grade, so my grandfather had only a sixth-grade education well into his late teens. Until then I had no idea that my grandfather had lived so far out in the sticks, so deep in the mountains.

Don told me that once, when my grandfather Ernest was young, he was out walking on a trail and came upon another young kid about his age walking in the opposite direction. The kid was carrying a Bible and he had some more Bibles in his bag. Ernest had an apple and he traded the apple for one of the kid's Bibles. Most of the families in this part of Arkansas were too poor to afford one, so this was a real coup. Ernest and this kid then got into some sort of scuffle for some reason. The kid insulted Ernest, who proceeded to beat up the kid and take back his apple, and he kept one of the Bibles, too.

I get such a kick out of this detail.

Ernest began reading the Bible. He could read at only a sixth-grade level, but that was good enough to make it through most of it and to figure it out. The Bible set him on fire. My grandfather was a Christian liberal badass kid living in the country.

He was reading the Bible from a pure standpoint, with no baggage of a church telling him what it was about. In his late teens Ernest decided he wanted to become a minister. He became a radical Christian, in favor of unions and supporting the poor as much as possible. Not everyone was born equal in terms of money. He wanted the poor to get more resources and he would do anything to try to make it happen.

He was ordained sometime in the 1920s. Then the Depression hit in 1929 and his passion for the poor and his denunciations of the rich grew even stronger. He met his wife and my dad was born in 1930, in the early days of the Depression.

Back then big land companies owned farms that had sharecroppers and tenant farmers running the farms and then giving the owners most of the proceeds. It was almost like slavery. Ernest hated this situation and he attacked it, using the Bible to back him up. We could use more of that today, really. Don told me that in 1947 my dad went to college with the intention of following in the footsteps of his father, but for some reason it didn't take for him. He didn't like it.

My father, Miller Williams.

Don appeared that night in Vancouver like a generous ghost, a spirit from another world. He helped me understand that my grandfather was more radical than I had known. If Woody Guthrie had been a minister, he might have been like my grandfather. That made me proud.

Like his parents, my father was always moving around, moving forward and moving ahead, moving here and there for this new job or that new job. Before he got his degree in biochemistry, he worked as a book salesman for Harcourt,

Brace, and he also sold encyclopedias door-to-door. You can see his early literary desires there. He always said he wanted to be a writer. As a boy he had written poems. Right after he finished high school, he went to Hendrix College in Conway, Arkansas, where he hoped to major in English, but as part of his entrance exam he had to take an aptitude test with a psychologist. His test results told him in no uncertain terms that he had absolutely no verbal aptitude and that if he didn't want to embarrass his parents he should go into science. Because he was taught to respect the opinions of his educational elders, he changed his major to biology. He pursued this course almost to a PhD. All along, his stubborn passion for writing and languages continued, until he found a way to make his dream come to fruition. Don Todd told me that my dad wrote him letters about his growing passion for poetry. He thought the poets were doing the same thing his father, Ernest, had been doing through his ministry—teaching something that was mostly hidden to the rest of the world.

Just like his father, my dad was always involved with fighting racial injustice. One of his closest and lifelong friends was George Haley, the brother of Alex Haley, the author of *Roots*. My dad met George in 1951, when he was a graduate student at the University of Arkansas and George was one of the first three black students to be admitted to the university's law school. George was being taunted and teased by some of the other students, so then my dad befriended him. My dad got called a "n—— lover" and they would get bags of urine thrown at them and experienced many other humiliating incidents when they were together.

Through all of this, my dad and George got to be really close, and when I was born, he asked George if he would be my godfather. George's brother Alex later wrote a beautiful piece in *Reader's Digest* that told their story, and of course I came into the world right at the end of it. One of my dearest possessions is a black-and-white photograph of George Haley holding me as a baby, which my dad gave me in this really pretty antique silver frame.

Me with George Haley.

When I say, "I'm a southerner," many people think, "That must mean you're racist, you're this, you're that." There are all these stereotypes associated with being southern, which is a whole problem in and of itself. I think that's why my dad instilled in me, "We are southerners, and we have to fight the people who think that all southerners are racist, all southerners are hicks, all southerners are stupid." That's how I was raised. That's my South.

One of my father's favorite stories was about when he met Hank Williams a few months before I was born, in January 1953. He went to see Hank play a show right there in Lake Charles, where my parents were living. He was bound and determined to meet him afterward. My dad adored Hank and his music, and I think, besides the shared last name, he just felt a kinship with him. They looked somewhat alike, too—tall and kind of lanky and gangly looking, with high cheekbones. It almost seems that they could have been related.

After Hank's show, my dad went up and introduced himself, and they ended up at a bar close to the venue, some place that Hank suggested. It was a gas station that served drinks; there were lots of places like that back then. The way my dad told the story, he and Hank were talking about how neither of them had any money growing up. He told Hank about being from Arkansas, a simple working-class family, his dad a Methodist preacher, and now he was a poet and a beatnik college professor. At some point Hank asked my dad what he wanted to drink and my dad asked for a bourbon and water. Hank said, "Williams, you ought to be drinking beer 'cuz you got a beer-drinkin' soul."

Hank meant that even though my father had gotten a college education and had become a professor, he was still connected to that part of the working-class world. My father would tell this story over and over. It might have been the most important lesson he ever taught me, to be able to accept and move in both the world you were born into and the world you found on your own.

A short time after that Hank died, and I was born three and a half weeks later.

2

My mother and my father were a good match on the surface of things and in the substance, too. She loved all the arts and was very supportive of my dad's passion for writing. Around 1961, we were living in Baton Rouge and my father was selling refrigerators at Sears, Roebuck, while trying to find teaching jobs in science. But what he really wanted to do was write. One night my mother and father went to a reading by the poet John Ciardi, who had done a famous translation of Dante's *Divine Comedy* among other things. After the reading there was a reception that they were not invited to, but people were too polite to kick them out. My mother went up to Mr. Ciardi and shook his hand and in the spur of the moment she said, "There is another great poet in this room tonight and you didn't even know it." He said, "Who is it? How could I not have known?" And she said, "His name is Miller Williams. He's my husband." My father was embarrassed by my mother's forwardness, but Mr. Ciardi asked my father to send him a few poems. Then a month later, after my dad had not yet sent them, John Ciardi sent him a letter saying, "Dear Mr. Williams, You were going to send me some poems—P.S. Tell your wife I like her way of going." This would prove to be a major turning point in my father's life as a writer. John became a mentor to my father and one of his lifelong best friends. I think I inherited some of my mother's fortitude that was on display in her willingness to go right up to Mr. Ciardi.

But sadly, my mother's illness was getting worse and she couldn't hold it together for very long. There were a few catastrophes. One time, when we were living in Baton Rouge, my father had a meeting with his dean from LSU in our living room. He thought my mother was asleep, and he invited the dean over for a drink rather than having the meeting in a more official space. In the middle of their meeting Mama wandered sloppily into the room extremely drunk, wearing only her underwear.

I was around nine years old and we were living in Baton Rouge when my mother had a terrible nervous breakdown, screaming and yelling at my father. This was not long after the John Ciardi reading, when she had been so supportive of him. You can see how her mental illness made her so unpredictable: Anything could happen, beautiful or horrible, at any given moment. One day she was kind and looking beautiful in her pants and a flowered shirt that buttoned up the front, with her hair done up nice. Then the next day she would spiral out of control, looking like a mess. I remember the ambulance coming and taking my mother away after that breakdown. I was trying to look through the blinds to see what was going on. This woman, I think one of our neighbors, had come into the house to take care of us while my parents were gone, and she told me, "Don't look. There's no reason to look." I remember that made me feel very angry. If I wanted to look, I should be able to look. I didn't want someone to tell me what I could or couldn't do at that time, especially not somebody I barely knew. If you can't look, you can't see.

When my parents were breaking up, my mother asked me who I wanted to stay with, her or my father. I don't remember answering. I probably wanted to stay with my dad. But I remember going into their closet and caressing their clothes, individually—my mother's dresses and my father's shirts. That was all I could do at that moment and somehow it brought me some comfort.

I cannot imagine how hard all this was for my father, who was only twenty-two years old when I was born. His wife was not able to be a reliable mother to his sick daughter.

He and I had a special bond. I believe I survived because of my bond with him.

Yes, my family was dysfunctional, fucked up. But that's not what really matters to me. What matters is that I inherited my musical talent from my mother and my writing ability from my father. My stepmother taught me how to set a table with cloth napkins and silverware for a dinner party. And Grandma Day taught me about mixing coffee grounds and eggshells to make fertilizer for plants and what banana pudding and fig pickles are supposed to taste like. And Mimmaw taught me church hymns and Pippaw taught me decency and diplomacy. In a way, my family was wonderful. Grandma Day crocheted pillowcases and my aunt Alexa (on my dad's side) kept track of every family member's birthday and always sent a card and sometimes one of her woven pot holders.

During those years, as my mother's mental illness was escalating, I spent a lot of time at Uncle Bob and Aunt Alexa's house. My cousin Mac would spend the night at a friend's house and I'd sleep in his bed. My dad would drop me off there and then he'd drop my brother, Robert, off at Grandma Day's house. Word has it that she spoiled Robert.

My uncle Bob was a part-time actor and was in various plays and musicals at the little theater in Baton Rouge. He made it possible for me to get a small part in a local production of *Annie Get Your Gun,* which was a popular musical for regional theaters in the 1960s. I fell in love with the stage during that production. This was a year or two before I started playing guitar. Being in front of an audience with other cast members, including my cousin Mac, Uncle Bob's son, I felt a high I'd never experienced before. I was hooked. Bob was always playing the soundtracks from musicals on his stereo at his house, too. I remember *Oklahoma!, South Pacific,* and others.

One of my earliest musical memories comes from an excursion my father took us on to get out of the house when my mother was spiraling. We were living in Macon, Georgia, and I was around five years old. Downtown Macon looked much like many southern downtowns back then, and probably still today. There was a long main street and side streets and the town was divided into a white section and a black section. There were huge antebellum mansions on the white side of downtown. There was a dime store and a barbershop and a soda shop. Imagine the town square in the movie *Back to the Future*, which is set around this time.

There was a blind preacher and street singer in Macon named Blind Pearly Brown. I'm not sure if my father knew him or if we just stumbled upon him when he was taking me to get ice cream or something. Brown was on the sidewalk playing a guitar and singing and collecting tips. I stood there holding my father's hand. It was a moment I would never forget. I loved the music so much that a few years later my father bought his album of songs recorded by the folklorist Harry Oster. When I got my first guitar, the songs on that album were some of the first ones I learned. Songs like "God Don't Ever Change" and "You're Gonna Need That Pure Religion," which at the time I didn't realize was a traditional song.

Years later I did some research on Blind Pearly Brown. In 1958 he was quoted by a reporter as saying, "I pray to the Lord that we will someday see a world without strife, when all of us can live as brothers. I hope the Lord lets me live to see the day when mankind is considerate of one another." In another article, in 1972, Brown was quoted saying, "It's not bad being a street singer. It will learn you something. You gotta look over how some people can be mean to you."

To me, this is the essence of the blues. It's about coming to grips with your experiences and learning something from them.

When we were living in Macon, my father took me to Flannery O'Connor's house in Milledgeville. I was eight years old. The firm that my father had sold books for, Harcourt, Brace, was the same firm that published some of O'Connor's books, so that's probably how he made that connection. In his determination to be a writer he had sought her out. He always considered her his greatest teacher. She responded by inviting him to visit. We drove up and there was a circular dirt driveway in front of the two-story house. As I remember it, there was a huge oak tree—a shade tree for the house—right in front or maybe just to the side. There was a screen porch along the front of the house.

When we arrived, the venetian blinds inside the screen porch on the front of her house went down. The housekeeper came out on the porch and said, "Miss Flannery isn't quite ready to receive guests." It was her writing time and she didn't want to be disturbed. The housekeeper told us that we had to wait until she was done. She said, "You can wait on the porch." This was very old-school southern. After a while the housekeeper came back out and said, "Okay, Miss Flannery is ready to see you. You can come in." My dad went inside and sat with her. While they visited, I stayed outside and wandered around her yard and chased her peacocks. It was years later that I learned how meaningful this visit was. I'm lucky that I retained that memory.

I knew that kind of southern gothic experience from spending time with my mother's side of the family, and I think that's why I loved Flannery O'Connor's writing so much. I first read her when I was sixteen, long after that visit, when I had been too young to appreciate anything about her writing. At sixteen, though, I found something that felt real. I started reading her short stories and I just inhaled them all. I understood what she was talking about immediately.

There was a state mental hospital in Milledgeville and the patients would be wandering all over her town. Flannery wasn't an elitist. What she was talking about was right in my own backyard as well. It wasn't anything unusual to me. The southern gothic was my everyday life.

The movie based on her novel *Wise Blood* is the best adaptation from a book into a film that I've ever seen. They didn't try to clean it up or sugarcoat it. It was filmed in Macon, Georgia. The n-word is in it. But that's how it was back then. That darkness, that imbalance.

O'Connor would become a mentor to my dad. A few years later she would help him get his position teaching English at Louisiana State University in Baton Rouge.

My childhood was such a mixed bag. I was exposed to people like Blind Pearly Brown and Flannery O'Connor and learned how to appreciate that the aesthetic sensibility of a person was something important, something that made them different and worth noting. But I also had to live with a tremendous amount of pain, both physically and mentally. I endured my mother's volatility and the incessant moving from house to house, town to town. Forty years later, when I was living in Nashville and enjoying some widespread notoriety in my career for the first time, I would write a song based on images from all those hours and days riding in the car from place to place, along with chaos and turmoil inside whatever house we were living in at the time. The song is called "Car Wheels on a Gravel Road."

> Sittin' in the kitchen, a house in Macon
> Loretta's singing on the radio
> Smell of coffee, eggs and bacon
> Car wheels on a gravel road
>
> Pull the curtains back and look outside
> Somebody somewhere I don't know
> Come on now, child, we're gonna go for a ride
> Car wheels on a gravel road . . .
>
> Can't find a damn thing in this place
> Nothing's where I left it before
> Set of keys and a dusty suitcase
> Car wheels on a gravel road

There goes the screen door slamming shut
You better do what you're told
When I get back this room better be picked up
Car wheels on a gravel road . . .

Low hum of voices in the front seat
Stories nobody knows
Got folks in Jackson we're going to meet
Car wheels on a gravel road

Cotton fields stretching miles and miles
Hank's voice on the radio
Telephone poles, trees, and wires fly on by
Car wheels on a gravel road . . .

Broken-down shacks, engine parts
Could tell a lie but my heart would know
Listen to the dogs barkin' in the yard
Car wheels on a gravel road

Child in the backseat 'bout four or five years
Lookin' out the window
Little bit of dirt mixed with tears
Car wheels on a gravel road

When I first started playing this song in public, my father attended one of my shows at the Bluebird in Nashville. It was the first time he heard the song. He came up to me afterward, wearing his standard college professor slacks, shirt and tie, and sport coat, slim as he always was, with his beard and glasses. He said, "I'm so sorry. I'm so, so sorry." I asked him what he meant, and he said, "That little girl crying in the backseat was you." It was a bittersweet moment I'll never forget. I was amazed and moved at the same time. I had not realized that I was writing about myself the entire time! It took a poet to show me.

Sometimes I wish I could be more intellectually savvy in my songwriting, the way Bob Dylan is. But all I can do is write about my feelings and the world's feelings, and I think maybe this is what makes my music unique. It borrows from southern gothic elements and blues and folk and rock.

I believe that if you're seriously to look into things—and if you're truly able to see—you're able to be wise and soulful. You don't have to have a formal education to be good at whatever it is you do. I had many conversations about this with my father. He never made me feel bad about not liking a certain writer or a certain artist. For example, I never liked Faulkner. I tried to read him and I just didn't like him. I preferred Flannery O'Connor and Carson McCullers. I was hesitant to tell my father this because Faulkner was so revered at the time. I finally told him and he said, "Oh, that's okay. You can read somebody else. There are lots of writers out there. You don't have to like all of them." Then he paused for a moment and said, "Plus, Faulkner was an asshole."

3

There was always music playing in my parents' house, and countless literary parties. One of the joys of my father's life was to have a party at our house after a reading. Whenever those parties got going, my father would break out the southern soul records like Wilson Pickett and Ray Charles. He loved Ray's album *Modern Sounds in Country and Western Music*. He also loved Chet Baker and John Coltrane and Bessie Smith and Lightnin' Hopkins. And of course the early Folkways records were essential. I remember going with my dad to visit some of his friends and they played two albums that ended up being very important to me: *Songs to Grow On volumes 1 and 2* by Woody Guthrie and Pete Seeger. You could hear their humor and wit in the lyrics. Even though they were children's songs, there was something really deep and special about them. Another crucial early record for me was *Joan Baez, Vol. 2,* which my mother introduced me to when I was around eight or nine years old.

My earliest memory of playing an instrument was on my mother's zither that she had from when she was a girl. It was the same shape as an Autoharp, but you played it on your lap. You slid sheet music underneath the strings and it would show you how to play a song, almost like tracing a picture underneath a sheet of blank paper. You'd play with your thumb on one hand and fingers on the other hand. I was just starting to search for something to play. I wanted to accompany myself so I could sing songs.

In 1964, when I was eleven years old, my family moved to Santiago, Chile, for a year. A few years later, when I was seventeen, we would spend a year in Mexico City, and these two years in Latino cultures made an imprint on me that lingers still today.

We went to Santiago because my father had won an Amy Lowell Traveling Scholarship in Poetry. He met and befriended the great Chilean poets Pablo Neruda and Nicanor Parra. My father was buying Chilean records and listening to local radio. Nicanor became a close friend of my father's and his sister was a famous musician, Violeta Parra, who would be best known in America for her song "Gracias a la vida," which Joan Baez recorded years later. Violeta played Chilean folk music on acoustic guitar and sang, but her influence extended beyond Chile. By the time we moved to Santiago, she'd already recorded several records, which Nicanor gave to my father. There's a documentary film that calls her "the mother of Latin American folk music."

Her music made a big impression on me. Here was this woman in her forties playing guitar and singing folk songs beautifully and powerfully. Joan Baez was really the only American woman I was aware of at the time who was working in that manner.

Me as a schoolgirl.

I had to wear a uniform in school there and I hated it at first. But that quickly changed as I fell in love with the place and the culture and the music. Those times in Chile were politically turbulent but what was happening didn't fully register with me until years after we left. Many surrounding countries were undergoing revolutions, but the unrest in Chile was just beginning, with the violence increasing in the coming years, eventually leading to the coup of Allende in 1973. I have always remembered the story of the singer-songwriter and activist Víctor Jara, who was captured by the death squads. His fingers were chopped off before he was murdered. It was one of the most horrific things I had ever heard.

Unfortunately, Violeta took her own life in 1967 after her lover was killed in the revolution. She killed herself with a gunshot at forty-nine years old. My father first learned of her death from Nicanor. Now, looking back, you can see that the lyrics of "Gracias a la vida," recorded less than a year before her death, could be a suicide note:

> Gracias a la vida que me ha dado tanto
> Me dio dos luceros que cuando los abro
> Perfecto distingo lo negro del blanco
> Y en el alto cielo su fondo estrellado
> Y en las multitudes el hombre que yo amo

Translated into English:

> Thanks to life, which has given me so much
> It gave me two bright stars that when I open
> them,

I perfectly distinguish black from white

And in the sky above, its starry backdrop

And in the multitudes the man I love

I didn't know Violeta personally, but her brother Nicanor visited us in the States a couple of times. So it felt like I knew her, or I was one degree away from her. She was the first person I was related to in some manner who committed suicide, but sadly she was not the last.

At the end of my father's fellowship year in Santiago, we moved back to Baton Rouge. I was quickly in for some trouble. In Chile all the girls wore pants that were like tights, with no skirt over them. I had several pairs of those pants, but when I wore them to school in Baton Rouge, I was told to go home and change my clothes because my pants were too tight. The principals and teachers thought there was something naughty about those pants. In Santiago they were perfectly fine.

The first year back in Baton Rouge my father met my future stepmother, Jordan. She was an undergraduate in one of his classes at LSU. He was thirty-five years old and she was eighteen or nineteen. I was twelve. My sister, Karyn, was eight and my brother, Robert, was ten.

I felt so protective of my younger siblings at the time. My parents weren't separated yet, and my mother was still living in the house. Jordan came into the house as an extra guardian or babysitter and nothing was the same after that. It was a very strange and uncomfortable situation, to say the least. I have pictures of my mother and Jordan in the same room, hanging out, sitting at the dining room table. The sense was, *Jordan is going to come into the house and take care of the kids and save the family,* which of course my mother resented. You could tell something was going on between my father and Jordan and that she wasn't just a professional housekeeper or nanny. It wasn't normal. Here's this young girl, one of my father's college students, and she's only six or seven years older than me, and something is going on between them. But I didn't want to blame my father, because he had been my rock. I had to hold on to something. I just tried to be as respectful as possible and ignore the questions I was turning over in my head. But it wasn't easy.

Mom and Jordan.

Jordan was so young: she wasn't mature enough to handle the situation, either. Over the years, a couple of my therapists have told me they believe I harbor huge amounts of unexpressed anger toward my father about what happened with Jordan, but I didn't express that, because I didn't want to rock the boat. Kids can't understand what they're feeling. What did I do wrong? Who should I get mad at? I was stuck, and very confused.

My obsessive-compulsive disorder started the same year that Jordan entered our house. That was when I began to pick at my skin. Adolescent hormones were probably starting to kick in as well. I wasn't a cutter, as Dusty Springfield described herself being in her autobiography, but I created some cuts and sores.

One day my father took us on one of his excursions outside the house to get away from my mother, who was having a meltdown. I can't remember if it was just me or if my brother and sister were with us. It's possible he dumped them off with friends who were sitters. I don't know. Anyway, he took me to the drive-in and the first movie was *I Was a Teenage Werewolf* with Michael Landon and the main feature was *Hush . . . Hush, Sweet Charlotte* with Bette Davis. Both of those movies scared the shit out of me, especially *Hush . . . Hush, Sweet Charlotte,* in which somebody's hand gets severed from their arm by a cleaver and Charlotte—Bette Davis—has blood all over her dress. Then there's talk of decapitations and Charlotte gets drugged and has hallucinations.

What kind of dad would take a twelve-year-old daughter to see movies like this? I know he was desperate to get us out of the house because of my mother. As I grew older, I came to love *Hush . . . Hush, Sweet Charlotte* because it depicted the gothic South as I knew it from my mother's evangelical family, but instead of being in that house in Baton Rouge, it was set in a stereotypical southern mansion. Same dysfunctional crazy scary stuff hidden inside a grand mansion, filmed just a few blocks away from where all this shit had happened in my mother's family's house.

Nineteen sixty-five was also the year I got my first guitar and started taking lessons. I can't overstate how volatile that year was to me. I was on the cusp of being a teenager and all that brings on for any girl, and Jordan was now part of the family; I was experiencing a cauldron of feelings and desires. My teacher was a guitarist in Baton Rouge who played in a rock band. Years later, as an adult, I couldn't remember his name, but I had a picture of him. When I was researching this book, I posted that photograph on social media and some friends and fans helped me track him down. His name is Alan Jokinen and he lives in San Francisco now. In Baton Rouge he had been a graduate student in poetry at LSU and studied with my father. He was studying poetry in the daytime and playing in rock bands at night.

I remember Alan coming over to our house once a week. He had long blond hair and a rocker look. He was a gentle and sensitive man. We would sit there in the living room, and I would tell him a song I wanted to learn and he would show me how to play it. He taught me a rolling, fingerpicking style that I still use today. When I was working on this book, Alan told me that it was my idea to learn to play this way. He said I told him I wanted to play folk songs. The first one I learned was "Freight Train" by Elizabeth Cotten. She used the fingerpicking style in kind of a Piedmont blues style. I was really into Peter, Paul and Mary, so I learned how to play "Puff the Magic Dragon." Alan showed me chords and the fingerpicking techniques for any particular song that I chose, and then the rest of the week I would practice that one song. Then I'd be ready with another song for him to teach me the next week and he'd show me how to play that one. My goal wasn't to become an expert guitar player but to learn how to play songs so I could sing them.

Playing guitar for Mom and my brother, Robert.

When Alan and I reconnected in 2020, he told me that not long after my lessons with him ended and he finished graduate school, a professor hired him to drive his car from Fayetteville to San Francisco. The professor had gotten a new teaching job in the Bay Area. His family flew to San Francisco and Alan drove their car across the country. He dropped off the car and planned to stay in San Francisco for a few more days. As it turned out, he never left. He got a job there in a silk-screening business and eventually opened his own silk-screening shop. He made posters for Bill Graham and the Fillmore and others. He's retired and still living there today.

After Alan taught me to play, I would go to music stores and look for songbooks. I was always on the hunt. It was the only way I could learn because I didn't know how to read music. If I had a particular album and I found its songbook somewhere, I would get terribly excited. I can still remember that feeling of buying the songbook and then the intense desire to get home immediately. I'd learn the chords and the lyrics from the songbook and the melody by listening to the album. Some of my favorites were Joan Baez's *Vol. 2,* Judy Collins's *Wildflowers,* and *Beatles '65.* There was also the *Folk Song USA* songbook, which was kind of the folksingers' bible of those times and which I still have. It's this really thick paperback of American folk songs with English and Irish heritage, compiled by John and Alan Lomax. The book's subtitle is *The 111 Best American Ballads.* It has songs like "John Henry," "Skip to My Lou," "Little Brown Jug," "Down in the Valley," and "Oh! Susanna."

In the fall semester of that year, another student of my father's came over to the house. He walked in holding an album and said, "Oh my God, you need to be listening to this." He put it on our turntable. It was the new Bob Dylan album, *Highway 61 Revisited,* which was released at the end of August 1965. It completely blew my mind. I didn't understand the lyrics or the song titles—"Just Like Tom Thumb's Blues," "Queen Jane Approximately," "Ballad of a Thin Man." What does that mean to a twelve-year-old girl? It didn't matter. It struck me like a bolt of lightning and I can listen to that record today and still get that feeling.

Playing guitar for Mom.

I had never heard Bob Dylan before, but I had heard Woody Guthrie and I knew about the literary world of poetry through my dad. Poetry was suddenly merging with kick-ass rock and roll on this album. Dylan had borrowed from all these worlds and brought them together for the first time. I was completely mesmerized. I loved the cover of the album, too, with his hair and the mysterious guy standing there with a camera. That was it for me. Between that record and Joan Baez with her jeans and little T-shirt and bare feet and long hair, I knew this was what I wanted to be. As early as twelve years old, I knew I wanted to be in that world.

Can you fall in love with someone you haven't met? It might not be called love but it's something akin to that, I'm sure. I'm one in a long line of men and women who have been touched deeply by Dylan. He was my mentor, my musical soulmate. Of course, he wasn't aware of any of this but that didn't matter. I could dream. After that introduction to *Highway 61 Revisited,* I set about absorbing all his other albums, *Another Side of Bob Dylan* and *The Freewheelin' Bob Dylan.* He was my constant companion in a way, my shadow, or I was his shadow. I wanted to be him somehow. I wanted to do what he was doing. I learned to play "Blowin' in the Wind" and "Don't Think Twice, It's All Right" very early. Also, his song "To Ramona," which might be my favorite Dylan song of all. It's a song of love for a woman. "Ramona come closer, shut softly your watery eyes." He could have said "eyes," but he says "watery eyes." That one word makes a night-and-day difference. It implies that this woman had been crying or beginning to cry. I also love the melody, its Spanish flavor.

As soon as I learned how to play my guitar, pretty much all my free time was spent sitting around learning these songs. I'm still doing that today. From age twelve to seventy I've been doing pretty much the same thing, and I love it. It's the world I wanted to be in, a better world than the one I was in.

4

A year or a year and a half later, in 1966 or 1967, Dad got a teaching job at Loyola in New Orleans and we packed up and moved yet again. I was thirteen or fourteen years old. By now my parents had divorced and Jordan was soon to be my stepmother. Mama moved to New Orleans, too, but she had her own place. My sister and brother and I stayed with my father and Jordan, but we'd visit my mother regularly. At the time, I couldn't have articulated how messed up and confusing it was for us kids. It was the only thing I knew. I guess when you grow up in a certain environment, even if part of you knows otherwise, you sort of think everybody else is living like this. But it was a pretty big deal in the late 1960s when your parents got divorced. Everyone would ask, "Why are you living with your dad? How come you're not with your mom?" There was a certain kind of shame associated with not living with your mom.

We moved to New Orleans at the right time for me, though. For a teenager in love with music, it was the perfect place. There's a Neil Young song where he sings, "All my changes were there." He's talking about growing up in Canada. That's how I feel about my years in New Orleans aged about fourteen to sixteen. You can't imagine the amount of music, and the variety of music, that was feeding into my head. For this music to come to me at such an impressionable age, when my young girl's body and soul were starting to change so much, spurred a wild mix of happenings in my head and my heart, some weird, some good, some maybe not so good.

In New Orleans, I had guy friends mostly, and we all just loved music; it was our anchor. I couldn't find many girls who wanted to play music. I spent a lot of time hanging out at a house on Lowerline Street in Uptown near Tulane, where two brothers, David and Cranston Clements, lived. I was dating a guy named Fielding Henderson who played guitar with them in some high school bands and he introduced me to them. I thought they were important because Fielding said so.

I listened to every word he said. We loved each other and all we cared about was music and saving the world. We walked all over New Orleans talking about current events and cultural conflicts and the last record we'd heard. We had so much still to learn. We were hungry for knowledge. When Fielding introduced me to David and Cranston, I knew they were kindred souls.

Standing in front of our family's house
on Robert Street in New Orleans.

My family's house was on Robert Street in the Freret neighborhood and I could walk about fifteen blocks down Willow Street to get to David and Cranston's. Soon they became more important to me than Fielding. Their father was an architect and had built their house, which was a square mid-century modern house, but their parents had

also split and they lived with their mother. She was a beat-
nik, a cool mom. She worked all day as a secretary at Tulane
and she wasn't strict; she didn't yell at us if somebody
fucked up. Their house was a free territory. We could go
over there and hang out in David and Cranston's bedroom.
We'd light up a joint and listen to Zeppelin or Buffalo
Springfield or the Doors' first album, or *Surrealistic Pillow* by
Jefferson Airplane, or Dylan, or the Band, or Neil Young.
We'd listen to everything. The Beatles, the Stones, Hendrix.
David and Cranston's mom would come home from work
with a six-pack of Budweiser or Dixie beer and a pack of
cigarettes and she'd stay in the background. There weren't
all these rules. We'd leave the house baked and spend hours
walking down the sidewalks of New Orleans—Lowerline,
Maple Street, Decatur Street, the Quarter, everywhere.

David and Cranston both played in high school bands
and they knew a lot of other kids who were into music.
Sometimes there would be thirty teenagers over at their
house listening to music and smoking pot and drinking beer,
although it was mostly dope. If you were underage, it was
easier to find weed than to buy alcohol.

The listening experience was very serious, almost religious. We'd put on one album and everybody would sit there
and listen to the whole thing and not say a word until the side
was over. Rock music was everything to most of the kids
there, but I had my acoustic blues and folk and roots background and I introduced that element into the mix.

There was a schism in New Orleans at that time. And

maybe there still is today, and not just in New Orleans. This was the 1960s and there was Vietnam and the assassinations and integration. Everything was polarized. You had the group that hated the counterculture—the conservative business and civic leaders and the churchgoing types—and you had the group that embraced it. We were of course in the group that embraced it.

Sometimes we would skip school in order to listen to a new record. Or we'd take the streetcar on St. Charles into downtown. There was a variety store called Weinstein's that sold records and another store called Smith's Record Center. Whenever we had any money, we'd buy records. We would hang out in the French Quarter. We were teenagers walking around observing everything, taking it all in. There was a place called Buster Holmes' Bar and Restaurant. Clarence "Buster" Holmes was the undisputed king of red beans and rice. Going there was a rite of passage for anyone growing up in New Orleans. David and Cranston and I would find seventy-five cents and we'd walk up to the take-out screen window at Buster's and we'd get three plates of red beans and rice for twenty-five cents apiece. We'd sit there on the sidewalk and eat.

One of my fondest memories of that time was when my dad used to take us to Preservation Hall to hear a woman named Sweet Emma play piano and sing. It gave me a sense of what it might have been like listening to Memphis Minnie back in the 1930s and 1940s. Sweet Emma played very unpolished jazz and blues songs. There was no air-conditioning and I'd sit there listening to her and sweat. Sweating through your clothes is normal for New Orleans people.

Me in New Orleans.

One day when we were wandering around the Quarter, Jimi Hendrix came riding through on a flatbed truck, throwing out Mardi Gras beads and promoting his upcoming show. I had to go. Needless to say, seeing Hendrix was a huge deal to me at age fourteen. I went with a girlfriend and my father dropped us off. The show was in the middle of a football field, Tulane University's football stadium. There was a makeshift stage on the field, and the crowd was huge, but the bleachers were far away from the stage. Nobody was allowed on the field except the band and the stagehands. It was hard to see the stage and there were no video screens like there are today. But it was unforgettable.

One night there was an especially huge crowd at David and Cranston's house and a number of black kids were hanging out. The crowd spilled out into the front yard and somebody called the police because there were black kids there. The police came over and shut down the party. When David and Cranston's father heard about it, he was furious that his sons were hanging out with black kids. He tried to straighten them out. He forced them to move out of their mother's house and in with him and their stepmother. But it didn't take. They rebelled. They were expelled from high school and a friend of theirs stole his father's car and they all left town intending to drive to California. Each of them had saved his allowance for the trip but they still barely had enough money to do anything. They got as far as El Paso, Texas, before they were picked up by police because one of them had stolen a bottle of Coca-Cola at a gas station.

My father, on the other hand, had always been progressive and politically oriented. As a teenager in New Orleans, I would stand in front of the grocery store and hand out "Boycott Grapes" leaflets for Cesar Chavez, and I'd take my guitar and play songs at demonstrations every chance I could. I learned all the protest songs, not just Dylan, but songs like "Universal Soldier" by Donovan. I was reading books like *Soul on Ice* by Eldridge Cleaver and *The Autobiography of Malcolm X*. Shit was on fire everywhere in the world. There were all the assassinations—JFK and RFK and MLK and Malcolm X. Kids were being shot by police for protesting the Vietnam War on college campuses. I'd watch footage of these events on the news and cry.

I got kicked out of high school twice for participating in demonstrations. At the time all the good schools in New Orleans were Catholic but I went to a public school called Fortier, pronounced "for-shay," a French name that everyone mispronounced "for-tee-er." It was in the Uptown area of New Orleans in a large four-story brick-and-limestone building with a grand main entrance of fifteen or twenty long steps up to three double doors. There were so many steps, the entrance to the school was actually on the second floor. Inside there were wood plank floors and small metal lockers. It was overcrowded and understaffed, and even though it had recently been integrated, the principal was a blatant racist.

I got kicked out for the first time before the bell rang one morning. A friend of mine asked if I would hand out leaflets from the Students for a Democratic Society around the campus. SDS leaflets were lists of grievances and demands put together by students. When a black kid and a white kid would get in a fight at school, the black kid would get sent home and the white kid wouldn't. We were demanding for that kind of unequal treatment to stop. I got caught handing out the leaflets and was sent to the assistant principal's office with two other kids. The assistant principal reprimanded us and told us to never do that again or we'd be kicked out of school.

We left the office and I told the other two kids, "I'm not going to say the Pledge of Allegiance when it comes on. Are you with me?" Every morning in homeroom the Pledge of Allegiance would come on over the loudspeaker. You were supposed to stand up and put your hand over your heart and say the pledge. I decided I would stand up, but I would not say the pledge or put my hand over my heart. My two friends agreed they wouldn't do it either. We got caught and were sent to the assistant principal's office again. He got right in our faces and asked us one by one:

"Did you say the Pledge of Allegiance?"

"No."

"Did you say the Pledge of Allegiance?"

"No."

"Did you say the Pledge of Allegiance?"

"No."

We were suspended indefinitely. When I got home, I told my dad what happened. He said, "Don't worry. We'll get an ACLU lawyer and get you back into school." He did and I was let back in school. "Try to stay out of trouble the rest of the year," my dad told me.

I tried to, I really did. But a few weeks later when I showed up at school one morning, a humongous protest against racism was under way, a big march around the school. The NAACP was there and SDS joined in. I was in my homeroom watching the march out the window. Some of the kids in my class were spitting out the window at the protesters. The teenagers in New Orleans back then were as divided as their parents. A couple of progressive friends of mine saw me in the window and yelled, "Come on down!" I couldn't resist. My blood was pumping and I was thinking, "I gotta go down there." So I ran out of homeroom and joined the march. The cops came and started throwing people into paddy wagons. I was able to get away and make it back home.

Everybody involved was suspended indefinitely. In order to be allowed back in school, you had to go to the principal's office and vow to never be in another demonstration again. There was no way I was doing that. My father agreed. He said, "The hell with that. You're not learning anything there anyway." So I was basically homeschooled the rest of the year. Dad was teaching at Loyola and he arranged for me to sit in on some classes there. This was the last schooling I ever had.

More than fifty years later I'm still in touch with David and Cranston. Whenever I'm in New Orleans, my husband, Tom, and I will hang out with them. David ended up opening a bar and it's now one of the most famous dive bars in New Orleans—Snake and Jake's Christmas Club Lounge. In a way, David re-created the old free-form house party from his youth by opening this bar. Cranston became a very successful guitarist, playing with everybody in New Orleans over the years, from Dr. John to the Nevilles to Irma Thomas. It's funny to me that the three of us were such fuck-heads as teenagers, and yet all of us made our way into careers doing something we care about.

Mama always managed to find these wonderful big old New Orleans apartments. One place was on Carrollton Avenue near St. Charles. It was easy to reach since the streetcar stopped right there at the corner. She always made her apartments warm and comfortable. She liked folk art from different countries and had some pieces from when we lived in Santiago. She had a great collection of records and I helped her add to it. One of her favorite albums was *Concert by the Sea* by Erroll Garner. She collected lots of sheet music that she kept in her piano bench and on top of her piano. The sheet music looked like a magical mystery to me.

My brother, Robert, was often at our mother's place and he would play piano. He was quite good and would play for hours on end. Mama loved Judy Garland and Sammy Davis Jr. I think she identified with Garland's personal struggles, which were well known. But at the time I was so young and involved in my own life that I couldn't see that her mental health was that bad. Maybe I blocked it out to some degree because I had never known her as someone who would be there for me in a predictable manner. My relationship with her was positive, but she was almost like a ghost of a mother—there, but not really there.

But I loved her with all my heart. We would go thrift shopping together sometimes. Mama loved a good bargain and she was proud of the collection of furniture she'd found at the local St. Vincent de Paul thrift store. She had a great sense of humor and could make a lifelong friend within five minutes of meeting someone. It could be the woman at the bakery or the mechanic at the auto repair shop.

I felt good being able to help her in her later years as I became more financially stable. I helped her get a car one year. Eventually her health worsened and I had to help move her into an assisted living place I found in Fayetteville, Arkansas, which she grew to like. Robert and Karyn were there, as well as Dad and Mama Jordan, so they could keep an eye on her. Dad and Mama Jordan never turned their backs on my mother. I admire that about them. Whatever bad things had happened were always forgiven.

5

In 1970 my family packed up and moved to Mexico City for a year. My father had some sort of fellowship at a university there. We rented a two-story yellow house in the Distrito Federal part of town. The house came with a housekeeper who lived out back with her daughter. I would have been a junior, but I wasn't able to get into high school there. If I remember things correctly, I wasn't allowed into school because I couldn't get my proper papers together due to being kicked out of high school in New Orleans.

As a result, I spent most of that year just playing guitar. I wasn't really interested in anything else anyway. If I wasn't interested in something, I wouldn't do it. In high school I absolutely hated PE class, so I would just sit on the sidelines and take zeros. But if I was interested in something, like guitar, I was willing to work on it all the time, all day, every day. When I wasn't playing guitar, I was reading good literature. I remember reading *The Stranger* by Camus while we were living in Mexico City. But mostly I just played guitar and listened to records.

A year or so before we moved to Mexico City, trouble had erupted during political demonstrations there. The demonstrators had been given permission from the government to protest, but then the military and police surrounded them and opened fire. People were either killed or hauled away.

Me in Mexico City.

The year we lived there, we met a lot of people who had friends or relatives who were missing and they didn't know what happened to them. That felt scary to me.

There was a little park not too far from our house and I met some of the young hippie-type locals there. I'd hang out with them and smoke pot. They were always trying to get me to go to Oaxaca for the mushrooms. I met one good-looking Mexican guy who didn't speak English, so we talked only in Spanish. He kept saying to me things like "tener sexo" and "quiero tener sexo." I hadn't had sex yet, and my dad was terrified that I was going to get pregnant, or that I was going to get arrested for smoking pot and he'd lose his fellowship and we'd all be deported. But thankfully none of that happened.

One evening my father took us to a restaurant in Mexico City. It was fairly rare for the whole family to go out to eat. This was a place highly recommended to my father. The waiter explained that he would like to introduce us to a dish that was considered a delicacy in Mexico—*criadillas*, or "bull's balls" in English. None of us wanted to partake, but also we didn't want to appear rude in turning him down. My sister, Karyn, was the brave one in the family and she was the first one to eat the dish. She became a dedicated vegetarian shortly after that and she's still a vegetarian today.

The politically leftist, younger, progressive liberals in Mexico City were anti-American because of Vietnam, so we had to try to break down that immediate instinctive barrier in order to make friends with them and it was a struggle. The people who weren't anti-American were stiff and conservative and not our types anyway, so we weren't able to have the literary house parties my father loved to throw. It was different from Santiago, where we had met many poets and other writers. For that whole year in Mexico, we invited all of our friends in the States to come visit us, and most of them did.

My mother wasn't able to visit, but I stayed in close touch with her by mail and telephone. In New Orleans she worked in the office of an insurance company doing clerical work, answering phones mostly. People would call with questions about policies and she would talk to them for a long time, making friends with the company's clients and customers. I would call her from Mexico and she would tell me about all the people she talked to, or she would write me about them in letters. Because it was insurance work, she heard so many stories about things that had happened to families from all walks of life, like accidents or fires or retirees losing pensions. She enjoyed hearing the stories and trying to help people; maybe it lightened her own sadness.

One of our visitors was a close family friend from New Orleans named Clark Jones who was a sweet and soft-spoken musician. He was kind of a younger Pete Seeger. He played guitar, banjo, dulcimer, Autoharp, and ukulele, and he knew every folk song in the book—all the songs that I wanted to learn how to play. He was a historian of folk music and it seemed like he could tell the story of America by playing old folk songs. He was around ten or fifteen years older than me, but we would sit around the house in Mexico City and play music all day long, playing one folk song after another.

Playing music with Clark Jones in Mexico City.

One night when Clark was there, my father had invited over two people who worked at the American embassy. Clark and I were playing folk songs and one of those two people said, "We should send Cindy"—yes, I was called Cindy then—"and Clark out on the road to play some shows around Mexico."

It turned out to be a monumental experience for me. The embassy and the U.S. Information Agency set up thirty shows around the country for us. We packed up Clark's car and drove all around Mexico, staying in hotels booked for us by the embassy. We played traditional American folk songs along with songs by Dylan and Peter, Paul and Mary, mostly at high schools or colleges. The government officials thought it was a way to try to spread American goodwill around Mexico at a time when America was not very popular, and that it would demonstrate to the Mexican people that America wasn't only about bombs and the military, that we had a folk cultural tradition not unlike theirs. The embassy called our show "Folk Music from Spiritual to Protest with Clark Jones and Cindy Williams."

This was the first time I had ever played live shows, the first time I'd played in front of an audience of strangers, and it was both nerve-racking and electrifying. I had spent my years aged twelve to seventeen playing guitar mostly by myself or in a living room with friends and family. Now I was standing up in front of an audience of a lot of people, sometimes with Clark in a duo and sometimes by myself.

I specifically remember playing a few shows in San Miguel de Allende, which is an artists' town in a beautiful area. The audience included painters and craftspeople and musicians and writers. I was blown away by how well we were treated. After the show I was presented with a bouquet of flowers.

The embassy publicized the tour extensively and there was media attention.

I've still got many clippings from the Mexican papers describing some of our shows. Everyone was appreciative that we were taking the time to go into high school cafeterias or small university halls and play these songs. Something about a teenage woman being with a humble older man was also appealing.

Mexico City show poster.

After touring with me for several months in Mexico, Clark moved to North Carolina, where he continued his educational folk music performances. He would send us clippings about his shows. He'd play for the state parks and YMCAs and civic shows. I remember one story was about how he'd learned all these songs from the coastal North Carolina fishing and crabbing traditions—old mariner songs, sea chanteys—and he played them over a summer at a public park near the beach. He told a history of the North Carolina coast through songs. Another time he put together a program of folk songs about plants and played them at the North Carolina Botanical Garden. I still have all these newspaper clippings about Clark in my scrapbooks.

When I look back over my life, I realize that I've had a series of guardian-angel-type figures who gently but securely helped me get my craft and career together. Clark was one of the first of these figures. He was a beautiful human being with a big, warm spirit. At a time I was supposed to be in high school, I was traveling around Mexico playing folk music with Clark. It was an education that no school could have given me.

6

I missed Woodstock. I just missed the Haight-Ashbury
thing in San Francisco. I missed the folk era in Greenwich
Village in New York. I knew about them but I was too young
to pack up and try to go be in any of these places and take
part.

But I got to witness a cool literary scene. Most summers
in the 1960s we would travel to Middlebury, Vermont, and
attend the Bread Loaf Writers' Conference, which is like the
Woodstock of writers' conferences. John Ciardi directed it
for a while and he brought my father into the fold and put
him on the faculty. All the student writers stayed in these old
dorms and the faculty stayed in log cabins down the road
with their families in a rural area away from the main part

of campus. During the day there were workshops where younger writers would have their work critiqued, followed by free time to work in the afternoon. In the evenings everyone would meet at a place called the Barn, which was a big old building with a huge fireplace. In between readings by the established writers, there was basically one big party with everybody drinking and reveling together. Younger writers had to go through a rigorous application process to be invited to Bread Loaf. It was a big deal for them, and also for me at age sixteen or seventeen, coming out of my difficult high school experiences in New Orleans. Being at Bread Loaf was a higher level of something, although I'm sure that at the time I could not have said a higher level of what.

I developed an attraction to a couple of different poets during those years. One year I became particularly fascinated with a poet named John who had blondish hair. We hung out a bit during the party times at night. Nothing happened between us except long talks about music and literature, but those conversations were important to me. We stayed in touch by writing letters and we'd see each other again at Bread Loaf the next summer. He was real quiet and sensitive, a very artistic type.

A few years later I was living in San Francisco—this must have been 1974, so I would have been twenty-one—and I got a call from a mutual friend I'd also met at Bread Loaf who said, "John took his own life."

"What happened?" I asked.

"Oh, he was just too sensitive for this world," she said.

I remember thinking, "Bullshit, I'm not buying that explanation." This was the first person I knew fairly well on a personal level who'd committed suicide. I started writing down notes about it and I thought back to Violeta Parra. It woke me up to the reality that certain people simply decide they don't like what is going on, so they check out. I was thinking about things that would show up in my songs many years later.

Those summers at Bread Loaf were blissful, but something awful happened to me during one visit. I was sixteen or seventeen. I think it was 1970, the year we were in Mexico, and we came back to the States for Bread Loaf and then went back to Mexico.

One afternoon, in broad daylight, I was walking along the road. The area in Vermont was bucolic and beautiful and nobody thought it was dangerous for me to walk back and forth from the Barn to our cabin by myself.

But that day, a man, probably in his twenties, pulled his car over next to me. He got out and asked for directions or something like that. I was caught off guard. Then, the next thing I knew, he pulled me into a ravine beside the road. He pushed me down onto the ground. I was facedown and he was sitting on top of me trying to pull my clothes off. It was so surreal. He was struggling like he was wrestling me or fighting me. I knew he was going to rape me. All I could think was, "I hope he doesn't kill me" and "I hope he doesn't have a knife and stab me." Then suddenly something happened to me—my fight, flight, or freeze system kicked in, unconsciously—and I became completely still. I said to him in a calm voice, "Would you please get off me?" This was not something I did consciously. It just happened. When I said that, he got up and started profusely apologizing. "I'm sorry, I'm sorry." Then he asked me if I needed a ride to where I was going. I said, "No."

He drove off and I walked back to the Barn, where my father was. I remember walking up to where he was sitting with other writers, talking and having a drink. I whispered into his ear, "Don't let Karyn walk by herself outside." My sister was around twelve at the time. He said, "What are you talking about?" I told him what had happened.

My father called the police and I tried to describe the man and his car, which I remembered as vintage looking. Nothing ever happened. The police never caught anybody. For a long time after that attack I had very uncomfortable feelings—shivering, shaking, upset stomach—whenever I saw an old vintage car that looked like the one this man drove.

Another time, when I was in my twenties, I was driving on the highway and my car broke down. A man was walking toward me and at first I thought he was coming over to help, but as he got closer, I could see he had this huge erection sticking out of his pants. I jumped into the car and locked the doors. He just stood there with this erection outside my window and he was asking if I needed help. Finally he left.

I was traumatized by these incidents. A mark or a wound

was inflicted on me. I was left a little more afraid, a little more distrustful. But it pales in comparison to what my mother went through. Now that I know more about what happened to her when she was a kid, I'm surprised that she held it together as well as she did.

I was eighteen years old in 1971, when we returned from Mexico and my father achieved tenure at the University of Arkansas in Fayetteville. He had finally made it. He was settled. After moving to twelve different towns over the first eighteen years of my life, my father and Jordan bought a house in Fayetteville and lived there the rest of their lives. Jordan is still living there today. She's been in that house for fifty years.

My father and Jordan.

My father and a writer named Bill Harrison founded an MFA program at the university there and it became one of the top writing programs in the South and probably the country. Another writer named Jim Whitehead was an important part of the program. Every writer in the country, it seemed, came through for readings and workshops. The program had a budget to bring everybody into town. I remember James Dickey and John Stone and John Little being there.

My dad would actually hold the workshops in our house. It was kind of like a miniature Bread Loaf. I was lucky enough to be there and sit in, watching and observing. Sitting in on those workshops, I learned more than I ever would have learned in high school or college about writing and crafting words and images in sequences. I learned about the struggle of writers, how hard it is to write anything—a poem or a short story or a song or anything else—and then to stand up in front of a crowd and expose your work so publicly.

The workshops turned into parties at 5:00 P.M. That's when they'd break out the booze and the weed and whatever else and start cranking music on the stereo. The great thing about a town like Fayetteville is you could call friends at 3:00 P.M. and say, "We're having a party at 5:00 P.M.," and everybody would show up. Five o'clock was the magical hour when it was okay to start drinking. I've never experienced anything like that since then and I've been in a lot of places as a musician and artist. Nothing compares with that wild

Fayetteville drinking and partying literary scene. People think musicians are wild and crazy and drunk and fucking each other all the time. Musicians are nothing like writers, not even close, from what I've seen.

My father pouring a martini.

You can read about this in Charles Bukowski's book *Women,* where he talks about visiting the University of Arkansas to give a reading and a workshop. He doesn't name names, but the parties he writes about were at our house. Bukowski describes how he left the main party room and went into a little room downstairs where there was a double bed and he fucked another writer, and I'm sure the writer might have been a student. That's the same bed I used to sleep on when I was visiting my father and Jordan years later. Jimmy Carter actually slept in that bed, too, before he was president. He was in town for one reason or another and ended up at my dad's house.

In 1984, when I was thirty-one years old and had moved to Los Angeles, I decided to drive up to San Francisco and among other things I intended to try to find Charles Bukowski. I liked his writing and I had moved to California, so it seemed like a natural thing for me to do. I told my dad about it and he said, "Well, honey, you know that he'll probably try to screw you." Nobody uses that term anymore. How many fathers would say that to their thirty-one-year-old daughter?

When I think back on those days in my late teens and those literary workshops and parties at our house, one thing that comes to mind is that my father was in his forties at the time and Jordan was around twenty-three or twenty-four years old. My dad must have been kind of proud. He's got this young arm candy while he's hosting all these parties for the literati. That's what a lot of those male writers were looking for back then, even if they were married to someone else. Maybe they still do that today.

An aspect of my life that I think was a result of hanging around this wild scene as a teenager is that I had no desire to have my own kids. Never. It wasn't a gut-wrenching decision for me at all and I don't regret it today. I went on birth control at age eighteen and it never occurred to me to become a mother. Not once. When I was growing up, I never saw any families really enjoying their children. I remember thinking as a teenager, "Wow, nobody seems to like having kids. Nobody seems happy having kids. It's a burden, not a joy." It seemed like everybody would rather be partying and fucking each other freely. Family obligations and responsibilities didn't seem to be the most important thing to anyone, so why should they have been important to me?

Nowadays I look around and sometimes I get depressed when I see pregnant women or parents with young kids because I think, "Is this kid going to have a proper upbringing? Are these kids going to have a good education? Are these kids going to have good parents?" I don't know. I'm not judgmental about it. It's just a feeling about the challenges of parenthood that I first started having in my late teens, based on my own upbringing.

There was a steady flow of interesting guests at my father and stepmother's house. I liked that environment, and after I left home and was out on my own, I came to miss it, terribly. I tried to re-create it myself but I was never able to repeat it, not even with all the musicians I knew. I missed the literary world, the heady talks, the cocktails, the humor, the warmth, the savvy qualities, and the beauty.

Dad also started a poetry workshop at Cummins Unit prison in Gould, Arkansas. One day another writer, Bob Ward, was visiting us and Dad decided to have Bob and me go with him on one of his trips to the prison. I took my guitar and performed for the female inmates in the women's unit. It was a pretty rough prison where they would later perform executions. Needless to say, it was an unforgettable experience.

One of my favorite people to visit our house at that time was a woman named Louise. Her husband had taught art at the university. She was in her early nineties but still very youthful. I was mesmerized by her. She always visited during the Christmas holidays and she would drink gin and tonics and dance to Wilson Pickett playing on my father's stereo. What a constitution she must have had. She taught me that I could one day be in my nineties and still be beautiful and even sexy.

Louise lived with her husband in a cabin in the woods north of Fayetteville. Once I went to visit her while she was going through some of her things, cleaning out her closet. She gave me several pieces of jewelry and some barrettes for my hair. They were lovely pieces, turquoise and other natural stones. Someone later told me that she knew she was dying and she had invited me over to her house as a manner of saying goodbye. She passed away a few months later. I miss her deeply.

Even though I never finished high school, my father was able to get me admitted to the University of Arkansas, which I entered after we returned from Mexico. It didn't take, though. I lasted only one semester. Over Christmas in between semesters I went to New Orleans to visit my mother and I basically decided to stay there. I had found a joint called Andy's on Bourbon Street that was looking for singer-songwriters to play regular sets for tips. It was in the middle of all the strip clubs and tourist attractions. It was just a stool with a couple of microphones and they were open all night until dawn. Tourists would drop in and check it out. Artists would sign up to play certain time slots, like 8:00 P.M. to midnight or 9:00 P.M. to 1:00 A.M. I auditioned and got a regular time slot at Andy's. I was so excited. My first regular gig. I played sets for a couple of weeks and the money wasn't bad. It was enough to pay a month's rent, which was around eighty-five dollars a month to share a place with someone back then. I was supposed to return to the university but I called my dad and told him about this job. He said, "Honey, if you want to stay and do that instead of going back to school, that's fine with me." I was so happy. I always look back at that as a turning point in my life. What if my father had said, "No, you have to return to college"?

While playing at Andy's and sharing an apartment with a stripper, I became friends with some older guys who lived together in a big, rambling house. They invited me to a number of dinner parties where there was a lot of pot smoking. It was Hippie Central. One night I was at a dinner party and there was a woman sitting at the table across from me wearing no shirt. Completely topless. This was the 1970s and we were at the height of the women's liberation movement. It's hot and muggy in New Orleans, and if a guy could take his shirt off and hang out, why couldn't a woman do the same thing?

I actually never felt comfortable in that sort of environment. But of course I couldn't say anything, because I'd be seen as uptight and not free. The whole idea of freedom got way out of hand during those days. Women were putting themselves in awkward positions in the name of freedom. I knew what men were capable of.

I also remember being in that house and lying on a bed with a guy, smoking joints and listening to Nina Simone. The music and the pot smells wafted through the house. All the doors and windows were open. I was dreamily listening and I said, "I love Nina Simone's music. I hope to be able to do what she does one day." And he said, "You'll never be able to do that. You'll never be where she is." He was mocking. I left and never went back to that house.

Soon after that a sweet man named Zac entered my life. He was lanky and skinny with a full head of wavy blond locks and a big wide grin. He was childlike, in a fun way. We hung around together and goofed off all over New Orleans, which made him even more special to me. He didn't throw around a macho attitude or anything like that. He was all about love and peace and beauty, a true hippie, not a chauvinist posing as a hippie.

I had been wanting to try LSD for some time but I'd been advised to wait until I was eighteen years old. After my birthday Zac and I picked a day we would trip together. The acid was called orange sunshine. We spent the majority of the time in his room with the windows open, music playing, rolling around naked on his bed and on a blanket on the floor. We were hallucinating and giggling and playing with each other. We had no worries in the world. I loved it. I had my copy of the book *Be Here Now* by Ram Dass, the yogi and spiritual teacher who was popular back then. I carried that book everywhere I went, like it was a Bible. I was on a spiritual quest. I was exploring different paths, all sorts of religions, with the exception of Christianity, which I could not find a way to connect with. It was probably due to my father's pragmatic views. He called himself an agnostic, even though his father had been a Methodist minister. It could get a little bit confusing.

7

In 1972, I went to Nashville to audition at Opryland. A friend of my dad's, who was Tom T. Hall's bass player, arranged for me to come there and do the audition and put me up for a little while.

I didn't pass the audition but I had decided I wanted to hang around a little longer. I was going out to bars and one night I went to the Exit/In, which is still there. There was a whole little scene going on at the Exit/In; both Guy Clark and Townes Van Zandt were living in Nashville around that time and they were a part of that crowd. I also met a crazy guy named Wrecks Bell, who was a bass player, along with his sidekick, Mickey White, a guitar player. We got to be fast friends and they invited me to move into this big house where a bunch of musicians were living.

One night at the Exit/In, I met this musician and we invited him over to the house and we sat around and played music and drank Southern Comfort and smoked pot. All of a sudden the cops came to the door and we answered, and they came in and started to go through the entire house looking for pot, which they easily could have smelled. They found somebody's stash and a pot pipe in my room, so everybody got hauled in, except Wrecks, who somehow managed to get away. We got down to the station and eventually they let everybody go except me and this guy named Skinny Dennis, so we spent the night in the county slammer.

I remember that the musician Rodney Crowell got mixed up in all this too; I think he was about to move into the house, so he and a couple of the others who were living at the house were trying to raise bail for us. We did get out the next day—one night in that place was enough for me. But at this point my dad somehow was aware of what was happening—probably because I needed him to post bail. We got a lawyer, Rose Palermo, who had a reputation for being "understanding" to musicians.

Somehow Skinny Dennis decided he would take the rap, God bless him; he was older and I wasn't even twenty yet, so I guess he thought it wouldn't be that bad of a thing for him. Forty-plus years later, in 2012, I was crossing into Canada on tour and suddenly this pot bust showed up on my record. By this time I had been to Canada a thousand times before, and it had never been an issue. But that day it became a real issue; they were now giving me the third degree about what the arrest was actually for. They tried to trick me by asking how much pot was found in my room and I said, "None—it was just a pipe." I had to repeat that answer several times.

They said I needed to get ahold of someone in Nashville to prove that it wasn't a possession charge. Somehow my tour manager connected with somebody at Rose Palermo's office and they said that the records in Nashville were destroyed after a certain number of years and that arrest record was long gone. Apparently, that was enough to appease the border patrol. I still don't know how that would've popped up on my record after so long—especially since I didn't end up being charged with anything.

I guess the silver lining to the story is that a few years after we were arrested, Wrecks and Mickey would play on my *Happy Woman Blues* album.

One of the drawbacks of growing up the granddaughter of two church families is that I was riddled by this horrendous personal guilt all the time. So on the one hand you have all of this crazy southern gothic stuff going on in the background of my childhood, but then you also have southern Sunday church expectations to contend with. I didn't have a mother saying I should do this or do that or wear these proper clothes when you go out in public. My parents didn't do that. But the rigid, proper church culture was always there. The pressure of a certain ideal makes you feel really guilty if, like me, you come nowhere near approaching it.

And here I was, I never finished high school and I'm trying to be a professional musician in my twenties and I felt like a fuckup most of the time. Then, when you add the 1960s and 1970s hippie culture into the mix, I struggled to find where I fit in society.

Nobody was directly putting this pressure on me but I was feeling it. Maybe I put some of it on myself, or a lot of it. I remember all those New Age hippie books, and juice bars, and everybody becoming vegetarian. My mother introduced me to nutrition and yogurt. She told me about Adelle Davis, who was a pioneer in the health food movement. Her mantras were "Let's eat right to keep fit" and "You are what you eat." My mother wasn't pushing it on me; she was just telling me about it. It made some sense to me, but I also wasn't real sure.

I think that meeting some older blues musicians when I moved to Austin in 1974 started to liberate me from a lot of that southern Christian guilt and hippie bullshit that was very exclusive and limiting. I was dating a man named Rich Layton when he got the job to be sound engineer for a traveling blues revue called the Blues Caravan. The musicians were guys like Pinetop Perkins and Furry Lewis and Big Memphis Ma Rainey. I was invited to join them. I didn't play; I just tagged along.

Furry Lewis wore this suit coat with big deep pockets where he would keep a pint of whiskey. He carried the whiskey around all day and sipped from it like anybody else would sip out of their water bottle today. When the pint ran out, he'd get a new one. I'm watching him and I'm thinking, he doesn't give one fuck about drinking too much. He's just living his life. He was in his eighties. He'd been born in the 1890s. I was impressed by how carefree he seemed to be.

At this time, I was beating myself up with all these guilty thoughts, some of them real and some exaggerated in my mind: "I'm staying out too late, drinking too much, smoking cigarettes, eating too much sugar, eating too much fried chicken and barbecue, fucking my neighbor's ex-boyfriend, fucking this guy or that guy who I shouldn't be fucking." I was struggling with a lot of personal guilt. The thing about the blues is it tells you to embrace all of life, like "I've worked my ass off and I'm going to enjoy myself and not feel guilty about it." Every time I would start to beat myself up because I'd broken the rules, I would think about those blues guys and how they weren't worried about how much whiskey they were drinking or barbecue they were eating or how many

Austin around 1975.

cigarettes they've had or how many women they're fucking. There's something to be said for that freedom.

Around the same time I spent one night at Mance Lipscomb's house in Navasota, Texas, which is between Austin and Houston, in the middle of nowhere. Mance is one of the legends of Texas country blues. He was born in 1895 and lived in Navasota his whole life. He was born into a life of sharecropping and then he became a sharecropper himself.

I had been hanging out with this guy named Kurt Van Sickle who had taken on the role of managing Mance. Kurt was a singer and songwriter himself. He asked me if I would like to go along to meet Mance. Of course I would, I said, it would be an honor. I had been listening to Mance's recordings and learning from them for many years. So Kurt and I drove out toward his place and picked up Mance at a bus station. Mance wanted something to eat and he knew a greasy spoon that he said had great barbecue. So we stopped at this dive.

At the time I was working at a health food store in Austin and I was trying to eat well. Over the years I've worked in several health food stores and juice bars and I generally try to eat healthy food still today. But at the same time I now know I have to be careful that I'm not hard on myself for indulging in food that's considered unhealthy by some.

Well, Mance didn't give one fuck about healthy food, at least not on this particular day. We sat down and Mance ordered a huge plate of barbecue chicken with sides and several pieces of white bread. He was specific about the bread.

He wanted plain white bread, like Wonder bread. He's eating this greasy barbecue chicken and soaking up the greasy juices with the Wonder bread and loving every minute of it. Mance was nearly eighty at this time and skinny as a rail.

We left the restaurant and drove out to Mance's house. It was on the farm where he worked for most of his life. He also told us that he'd played Saturday night dances as a kid alongside his father, who played violin. Then he started playing those dances on his own or with his own combo in what he called "beer joints" and "juke joints."

We met Mance's wife. They had been together for something like sixty years. Mance was this tiny little guy and she was big and robust and had a loud deep voice. We ended up sitting around and playing music and singing songs.

A lot of these blues guys are insistent about what songs they've written that they didn't get credit for. They don't suffer fools gladly at all. Mance played "Key to the Highway" for us and he insisted that he had written that song back in the 1920s or 1930s. Today that song is considered public domain and is not credited to anybody. Big Bill Broonzy's version is the first one I heard and then of course Eric Clapton made it famous as a rock song. When Duane Allman died, "Key to the Highway" was played at his funeral in Macon, Georgia. Mance swore he wrote it. That night in his house he played a few other famous songs that he said he wrote and was never given credit for. I believed him.

The next morning, Kurt and I woke up and Mance's wife was cooking bacon and fried eggs and fried potatoes on the stove. It was the kind of breakfast the hippies said you were not supposed to eat. Granola and yogurt was the hippie breakfast. I remember watching Mance's wife cooking this breakfast for us and reflecting on how the whole hippie thing could be so intimidating and limiting in its own way. The blues guys taught me to be irrepressible, or encouraged me to honor my irrepressible streak.

I never finished high school, much less college, but I'm aware that everything I just wrote could be deemed part of this "noble savage" tendency that is discussed in academia. I see that. The thing is, my pain was real and I was processing my childhood pains for the first time. I identified with those blues musicians. Their lack of pretense stood in contrast to much of the social literary scene I'd experienced and enjoyed, to be honest, over the years. Also there was an inherent work ethic involved in being a blues musician. You can't learn to play this music unless you put in a shitload of time practicing it. Mance had been playing these songs his entire life. He wasn't trying to get something on his résumé or get accepted into anything. He was just playing these songs that he loved. That's what I wanted to do: to play songs that I wanted to play.

8

Through my teen years in the late 1960s my father was always adamant with me about cigarettes and sex and birth control. He told me, "I know a lot of teenagers are having sex already, but if you hold off on having sex until you are eighteen, then we'll get you the pill. And don't smoke cigarettes. They are bad for you." We had a little deal, and that's what I did. I didn't have sex until I was eighteen. After I started the pill, I didn't waste much time, though. Those were the days when you'd just go and go and go and go until the bed broke or something. The beds were cheap back then, at least the ones we were using at a young age. Some really funny things happened on those cheap beds and you'd go, "Oops." Those were the days of free love. I never did take to cigarettes, though, and I'm so glad I didn't because not smoking has helped my singing voice mature and grow long into my life and career. I feel today my singing is as strong as it has ever been. I don't sound like I did when I was younger; it's different, but just as good, at least to me.

I've been called an "erotic" songwriter. I don't disagree, but even though I had plenty of sex when I was younger, I was never promiscuous. I always had partners. Some of them didn't last that long, but I wasn't sleeping around willy-nilly. The brain is the real erogenous zone, at least for me, so I have to connect with somebody intellectually and almost spiritually in order to be attracted to them physically, and that rarely happens immediately. I realized early in my adult life that talking—real, honest, substantive conversation—could be superhot, and it didn't have to result in anybody taking their clothes off for it to be erotic in a lasting way, in a way that can really last longer in your mind and memory and in your feelings than physical sex. Very often a good conversation is more memorable than fucking. That's what I was getting at with my song "Something About What Happens When We Talk" on the *Sweet Old World* album.

As I was growing into a full-fledged woman, I began to be attracted to a certain kind of man, and I would maintain that kind of attraction for the rest of my adult life. The way I've often described this kind of man is that he would be "a poet on a motorcycle." These were men who could think very deeply and could have very deep feelings, but there was also a kind of blue-collar roughneck quality to them. The epitome of this kind of man for me was the poet Frank Stanford.

I met Frank sometime in the spring of 1978. I was twenty-five years old at the time. I had been living in Houston and Austin, plying my trade and craft in the music scenes in those towns, working odd jobs in restaurants and health food stores to pay my bills, but I was back and forth to Fayetteville to visit my father and Jordan (Momma J, as we came to call her) and sometimes I would stay there for weeks or a couple of months at a time. Dad's literary parties were in full swing at the house as usual and sometimes in the evening I would get out my guitar and play songs.

Frank had gone to the University of Arkansas in Fayetteville and studied poetry in my father's department, but I don't think he finished his degree. He was considered a legendary figure in the local literary circles in Fayetteville, but he never quite made a name outside that town. My father encouraged Frank to work on translations of poetry from foreign languages, but I'm not sure if their professional relationship was all that tight. Frank had already published a number of volumes of poetry by the time I met him, but he was working as a land surveyor to make ends meet. A land surveyor who wrote poetry . . . that's the kind of blend in a man that appeals to me.

Frank was twenty-nine years old and married to a beautiful, smart woman named Ginny Crouch who was a painter. Frank was also living, on the side, with another beautiful, smart woman, the poet Carolyn "C. D." Wright. He and Carolyn started a publishing company together in Fayetteville. It was a pretty weird situation, married to one and living with the other—an ad hoc, part-time commitment to both.

Frank was born in 1948 in a home for unwed mothers in rural Richton, Mississippi, and immediately put up for adoption. With his adopted family he grew up mostly in Greenville, Mississippi, and Memphis, and then spent his later teen years in Subiaco, Arkansas. He attended a Catholic high school on the grounds of the abbey there. His adoptive father owned a levee contracting company that built the levees on the Mississippi River, and they worked primarily on the levees on the Arkansas side. As a kid, Frank spent time in the levee camps down by the river, living with his family for months at a time among black laborers. Once an interviewer asked him, "What did you learn by growing up with black people?" and Frank answered, "How shitty white people are to them." The landscape and the culture of the rural South were in his blood and showed up in his poetry, which was carnal and gothic. There was a sense of death and danger and beauty present in his writing and in the way he lived his life.

When I met Frank, he had just written an epic poem called *The Battlefield Where the Moon Says I Love You*. Page 1 of that book contains these opening lines:

tonight the gars on the trees are swords in the
    hands of knights

the stars are like twenty-seven dancing Russians
    and the wind
is I am waving goodbye to the casket of my first
    mammy
well that black Cadillac drove right up to your
    front door
and the chauffeur was death
he knocked on the screen he said come on
    woman let's take a ride
he didn't even give you time to spit he didn't
    even let you
take the iron out of your hair
you said his fingernails was made out of water
    moccasin bones
and his teeth was hollow he was a eggsucker
you said he reached up under your dress and
    got the nation sack
you said the conjure didn't work he didn't smell
    the salt in your shoes
you said he came looking for you hid out in the
    out house you waited
for him with a butcher knife you asked him why
    not
let the good times roll
you wasn't studying about kicking no bucket
his tongue was a rattlesnake those sunglasses
    death wore

I was talking to the pew of deacons they had
    white gloves on
a midget collected ears on a piece of bob wire
the black dog lifted his leg on the hubcap
the wagon load of boots and banners was
    dumped in the bayou
the chain gang drowned together in the flood
the disguised butterfly
the quivering masts when the hero returns

It went on for 383 pages. His writing was feral and on fire. Everybody locally was proclaiming him the next great American poet. He knew a lot about blues and country music and I think his poetry came from that background, and was also part of the Flannery O'Connor southern gothic tradition.

I found him to be irresistible, and so did a lot of other women, and men, too. Everybody wanted to be around him. He was a cross between Jack Kerouac and a southern country boy. He was stocky, very fit, built like a wrestler or a rodeo man. He was charismatic and enigmatic, swashbuckling and sensitive at the same time. When you look at pictures of him, you can understand how women would fall in love with him. He was charming and magnetic, but there was also a certain sense of him being troubled, brooding sometimes, and unstable. He was married to another woman before Ginny, and I was told that he spent some time in a mental hospital after that divorce.

I was enamored of him, in love with him. I don't know what you would call our relationship. I wouldn't say it was a love triangle, or a love square, with me and Ginny and Carolyn, because Frank and I never actually had sex. We just hung out together and talked. He was genuinely attentive to what I had to say and he knew exactly what to say in response. He knew what I wanted to hear, which implies some manipulation, but it also suggests to me that he cared. We talked about poetry and lyrics and feelings and desires, all sorts of topics about caring about individuals and caring for the world, about how the world was fucked up and so hard on most people while some people had it easy, and why it was important to be a poet or a singer even if your audience was never going to be very big, which certainly seemed to be the case for me at the time.

My relationship with Frank lasted only about two months and then he killed himself by shooting a handgun into his chest. There are various versions of the events that led to his suicide.

Basically, all the stories overlap in claiming that Ginny and Carolyn had had enough of Frank's philandering and they confronted him together, almost like an intervention, and he couldn't handle it. He had left town for a couple of weeks before this happened. He might have gone to New Orleans, possibly to visit with the poet Ellen Gilchrist, who he was close to. He was always leaving town on what he said were land surveyor jobs, but Ginny and Carolyn came to find out that he was having affairs with women all over the region.

When he returned from this one particular trip, he found Ginny and Carolyn waiting for him. They told him they were onto his game and he had to choose one of them and stick with that one, or they were both leaving him. He went down the street to a friend's house and borrowed a pistol and then he came back to the house and shot himself. The whole thing resembled a Shakespearean tragedy.

Fairly recently, long after his death, I was playing a show in Dallas and Frank's sister, Ruth, attended the show and made her way backstage afterward. She had yet another take on Frank's death. "I have no regard or respect for Ginny or Carolyn," she told me. She thought they knew what they were getting into when they got involved with Frank. She felt that they had ambushed him. When Frank got back from that trip, they had covered his truck with women's underwear—bras and panties and lingerie. She thought they should have known that what they did was going to shame him and crush him. They had known that he'd spent time in a mental hospital after his first divorce. They weren't wrong to confront him, but they didn't need to do it so dramatically. Anyway, that's her version. Maybe she was being the protective sister.

Frank had sent me flowers to my father's house and they arrived on the day he killed himself. I don't know if he sent them on the same day or the day before or what. I got the flowers but I never saw him alive again. He had sent the flowers to let me know that he'd been thinking about me while he was gone.

My father was one of the first people Ginny and Carolyn called. They asked if he could come over and help clean up the bloody mess. My song "Pineola" pretty much tells the rest of the story from my point of view. I worked on this song for years and it was released in 1992, fourteen years after Frank's death. Sometimes it takes that long to get a song right.

> When Daddy told me what happened
> I couldn't believe what he just said
> Sonny shot himself with a .44
> And they found him lyin' on his bed
>
> I could not speak a single word
> No tears streamed down my face
> I just sat there on the living room couch
> Starin' off into space
>
> Mama and Daddy went over to the house
> To see what had to be done
> They took the sheets off of the bed
> And they went to call someone
>
> Some of us gathered at a friend's house
> To help each other ease the pain
> I just sat alone in a corner chair
> I couldn't say much of anything
>
> We drove on out to the country
> His friends all stood around

Subiaco Cemetery
That's where we lay him down

I saw his mama, she was standin' there
His sister, she was there too
I saw them look at us standin' around the grave
And not a soul they knew

Born and raised in Pineola
His mama believed in the Pentecost
She got the preacher to say some words
So his soul wouldn't be lost

Some of us, we stood in silence
Some bowed their heads and prayed
I think I must've picked up a handful of dust
And let it fall over his grave

I fictionalized a few details, but the song is true figuratively. In the Catholic Church if you kill yourself, you are screwed, you are going to hell, and you aren't given a funeral. Frank's mother was distraught and she insisted that he have a funeral and be buried by the Subiaco Abbey. She begged and pleaded with the Catholic diocese and finally they gave in. It was hard to include all that in "Pineola," so I changed Catholic to Pentecostal. I preferred the idea and the sound of that word.

The part about Frank's funeral that still haunts me today, and this is in "Pineola," is that there was a big turnout of his friends and followers, and his family didn't know any of them, and vice versa. Two different worlds of people came together for the first and only time at Frank's grave. I can't let go of that image.

I did pick up some dirt and toss it on the grave. It was a southern gothic story. A girl standing there with her little secret. There I was, and of course Ginny was there and Carolyn was there and Frank's mother and sister were there, and I was the only one who knew anything about how I felt about Frank. Later I heard that Ginny and Carolyn moved in with each other for a while after Frank's death. Another gothic twist to the story.

After my song came out and I was getting more notoriety in my career, the legend of Frank Stanford continued to grow. His books were published in new editions. People started researching him and his work. Some people have told me that my song caused that surge of interest in Frank, but I'm not sure about that. It might have been a coincidence. One time, probably thirty or thirty-five years after Frank died, a writer called me and told me that he'd been digging into Frank's papers at Yale University and that my name appears in them. He told me that Frank wrote, "I feel free. I've been hanging out with Lucinda and she makes me feel freer." That made me feel good, but it also was a bit unsettling. This writer intimated to me that Frank and I had had this tumultuous affair and that's not true.

Frank's suicide came four years after the suicide of my friend from Bread Loaf. Over the years my thoughts and feelings about those two deaths formed the basis of my song "Sweet Old World," which was also the title of the 1992 album that included "Pineola." It took a dozen or more years for me to finally get those two songs right and record them.

See what you lost when you left
This world, this sweet old world
See what you lost when you left
This world, this sweet old world

The breath from your own lips, the touch of
    fingertips
A sweet and tender kiss
The sound of a midnight train, wearing
    someone's ring
Someone calling your name
Somebody so warm cradled in your arm
Didn't you think you were worth anything? ...

Millions of us in love, promises made good
Your own flesh and blood
Looking for some truth, dancing with no shoes
The beat, the rhythm, the blues
The pounding of your heart's drum together with
Another one
Didn't you think anyone loved you?

See what you lost when you left
This world, this sweet old world

See what you lost when you left
This world, this sweet old world

There was an obituary of Frank in the free weekly paper in Fayetteville called *Grapevine*. I clipped it out and put it in my scrapbook and I still have it today. Along with the obituary, this poem of Frank's was published, which I also clipped and saved:

The Light the Dead See

There are many people who come back
After the doctor has smoothed the sheet
Around their body
And left the room to make his call.

They die but they live.

They are called the dead who lived through
    their deaths,
And among my people
They are considered wise and honest.

They float out of their bodies
And light in the ceiling like a moth,
Watching the efforts of everyone around them.

The voices and the images of the living
Fade away.

A roar sucks them under
The wheels of a darkness without pain.

Off in the distance
There is someone
Like a signalman swinging a lantern.

The light grows, a white flower.
It becomes very intense, like music.

They see the faces of those they loved,
The truly dead who speak kindly.

They see their father sitting in a field.
The harvest is over and his cane chair is
    mended.
There is a towel around his neck,
The odor of bay rum.
Then they see their mother
Standing behind him with a pair of shears.
The wind is blowing.
She is cutting his hair.

The dead have told these stories
To the living.

Just three weeks before Frank died, I had signed my first record contract. On May 12, 1978, I signed an agreement to make a record for Folkways Records for three hundred dollars.

9

The seeds for my Folkways record deal were planted when I was living in New Orleans back in 1972 and met another singer-songwriter named Jeff Ampolsk. We kept in touch and a few years later he recorded an album for Folkways. I was aware of this legendary label run by Mo Asch, which is now part of the Smithsonian, but I never thought I could record for them. Jeff and I were talking in early 1978 and he said to me, "If you send a cassette demo to Mo, I bet he will make a record by you."

I was incredulous, but Jeff urged me to do it and gave me the address. I made a cassette of the tunes that I had been playing in shows and I sent it to Mo. These songs were covers of classics by musicians such as Robert Johnson, Memphis Minnie, Hank Williams, and Sleepy John Estes.

Sure enough, a few weeks later, I received an offer from Mo to pay me three hundred dollars for a record. It was as simple as that. My first record deal, with a label that had released a lot of music I loved, the old folk and traditional tunes I'd been listening to since I was a kid. Now I just had to find a studio where I could make the record.

I signed my one-page contract with Folkways and I figured it was only right that I take the time to travel to New York City and meet the legendary Mo (short for "Moses") Asch. He turned out to be very friendly, but in a hard-boiled New Yorker kind of way. Despite his hard edge he had a good-natured grandfatherly way about him. I had the utmost respect for him and what he had done with the label. Folkways was to folk music what Blue Note was to jazz—iconic and respected. It was a very big deal for me to be recognized by Mo and Folkways. I knew they couldn't make me a star but I didn't care about that at all. I would become part of a family of artists and I felt like the label would take care of me.

Before Folkways could release my album, Mo told me I had to sign with a publishing company so that my original songs would be protected. At the time I was without a manager, a lawyer, a publisher, or a booking agent. I was just me. I was completely on my own, taking my own chances. I ended up signing a contract with a small company called Alpha Music, which Mo suggested. He said all the artists that signed with Folkways had publishing deals with Alpha. They had sort of a brother-sister relationship. That contract with Alpha would come back to haunt me in a manner that's almost humorous now.

When my father was an undergraduate at Millsaps College in Jackson, Mississippi, one of his best friends was a man named Tom Royals who would go on to become a civil rights attorney in Jackson. Tom had been a part of my life for as long as I could remember. He came to visit us quite often. In terms of his career and his personal presence, he was like Gregory Peck in *To Kill a Mockingbird*, kind and genteel and warm and thoughtful. He played guitar and sang a bit as a hobby. Whenever he came to our house, he'd bring his guitar and he and I would sit around and play and sing. He had a big heart, a warm laugh, and a sense of humor. He was one of my favorite people I've known in my entire life. His first marriage didn't result in any kids and he ended up remarrying and having two daughters as an older first-time dad, but at this time in 1978 he was single and I think he sort of took me on as a daughter.

Tom was one of these "guardian angels" who helped me at pivotal points in my career. When he learned about the offer I had from Folkways, he called me and said, "I know a fellow who's an engineer at Malaco Studios here in Jackson. I helped him get off a drug charge, so he kind of owes me a favor. Why don't I see if I can set up some studio time for you at Malaco and you can come here and make the record and stay at my house?"

Malaco was a legendary R&B and blues studio. Musicians like Bobby "Blue" Bland and Little Milton recorded there. (Sadly, it would be destroyed by a tornado in 2011.) I brought a guitarist named John Grimaudo from Houston and we stayed at Tom's house and cut that record in one afternoon. We recorded traditional covers that I'd been playing for years. That's what had been on my demo cassette and I figured that's what Folkways would want.

John went back to Houston and I ended up staying at Tom's house for several months into the fall of 1978. He welcomed me and he even gave me use of his MG sports car. I remember walking into his house one day and Tom was sitting there in the kitchen by himself eating boiled peanuts and boiled eggs. He was on an Atkins diet. He was so nice to me.

I played gigs wherever I could around Jackson and I met a Frenchman named Franck Madoeuf who was teaching French at a girls' school in town. One weekend in October of that year there was the inaugural Delta Blues Festival in Greenville, Mississippi. I drove over to the festival with Franck. Furry Lewis and Bukka White were among the musicians playing. Franck and I wandered around at the festival together and separately until we met back at the car to drive back to Jackson. While I was wandering, I met this young guy with a guitar. He was from Greenville and he seemed so young but he already was a Vietnam vet. He was one of these lonely, road-weary types that I'm drawn to. He told me about being traumatized by the war. In today's terms I suppose he would be said to have PTSD. We spent the day listening to the music and talking. Something about him left an impression on me. I never saw him again but we stayed in touch for a while by mail. The next day I started jotting notes for a song that became "Greenville," to be released twenty years later on *Car Wheels on a Gravel Road*.

My Folkways album was released later, in 1979, and I figured the best thing I could do was move to New York City. I lived there for about eight months, and that was about all I could handle. It was really hard to be there and be broke. By the time I got to the city, the exciting folk scene I'd always heard about—when Bob Dylan and Joan Baez were hanging out in the coffeehouses, and dreams were being made—was pretty much over, although there were still some of the classic venues up and running. There were some wonderful up-and-coming singer-songwriters around, too. Suzanne Vega was blowing the minds of everyone who had the opportunity to hear her performances. She was a pretty girl with interesting eyes and a mystery about her. She drew you into her orbit. Her way round a song was striking: she had mastered the art of economical and efficient songwriting—clean and without frills, no vibrato.

My friend Lynn Langham said I could contact her boy-friend when I got to the city and he would put me up in his apartment, which was located in the Little Italy neighbor-hood. He was a nice enough guy and would bow and say "Hi, y'all" when he saw me. Obviously, the word "y'all" refers to multiple people and shouldn't be said to one person. I think he addressed me that way because I was southern.

I had been to New York City before, but never on my own. I was determined to make it work and not be intimi-dated, yet there were always circumstances that could test your resolve. One time I went to a laundromat and while my clothes were in the dryer I went to get coffee. When I re-turned, I was dismayed to find that someone had stolen my clothes out of the dryer. But I carried on. I learned the sub-way system, often taking long rides to the outer boroughs to play at places like Flushing Local Coffeehouse. The rides were often longer than the time I got to play, and usually I would play to mostly empty rooms for ten to fifteen dollars.

Soon I moved into a sublet with a singer named Susan Osborn. We met on the street while she was busking. I was walking nearby and was drawn to her voice, which was one of the most beautiful I'd ever heard. She sang regularly with the Paul Winter Consort and they would sometimes perform at the Cathedral of St. John the Divine. She was a spiritual woman and we connected in that way too.

Eventually I moved into an apartment with two other roommates in the East Village, on First Avenue and Second

Street. I shared the apartment with a guy who crocheted all the time and a singer-songwriter named Marie. I remember coming home and having to step over a homeless man who was passed out on the steps leading up to our doorway. I also remember seeing these big round wooden spools on the streets that I think held telephone wire. The city must have left them behind knowing people would take them and use them for tables. Once I found one in our neighborhood and rolled it the three or four blocks to the apartment. It was a real prize at the time because they didn't last long on the street.

I became friends with the owner of Gerde's Folk City, Mike Porco, this little old Italian New Yorker who had taken a liking to my music. I signed up to be on the waiting list of performers to have a chance to fill a regular time slot on the stage at Folk City if one should open up. Occasionally, Mike would let me fill in for regulars when they couldn't make it.

One night after I finished my set at Folk City, I stepped off the stage and into the crowd toward the bar. Mike approached me and said, "Loooo-cinda, I want you to meet a friend of mine."

"Of course," I replied.

Then he turned around and faced the bar and pointed to a skinny, unobtrusive guy sitting on a barstool. We walked over and Mike says, "This is Bobby . . . Bobby Dylan."

I extended my hand, not half thinking at first, and then I realized what was happening and I froze. My hero was right

Playing at Gerde's Folk City.

there in front of me, looking at me. Just let me say that I felt the blood rushing through my body and through my heart to my head. I had this sensation that there was no one else in the room except me and Dylan. It's hard to describe because it's nothing like anything I had felt before or since. The kinetic energy was palpable. At a certain point, he had to leave, because being Bob Dylan, he couldn't keep hanging out. I decided to go stand by the door so that when he left he would see me. As he walked to the door, he leaned over and gave me a gentle kiss on the side of my face. He said to me, "Let's keep in touch. We're going to be going on the road again soon." I was in heaven. I walked on air back to my East Village apartment.

Two decades later Dylan's people approached me about opening shows for him and Van Morrison on a tour they were doing together. Hell yes, I'll do that, I said. We played a few months of shows together and I never had the op-portunity to speak with either Bob or Van the whole time. Maybe it's better that way. I have my memory of that perfect night.

10

A nother one of the guardian angel figures to emerge in
my life was a man named Hobart Taylor, who remains
a close friend today. I met him sometime in 1976, two years
before my Folkways deal, when I was living in Houston playing at Anderson Fair and other joints in Houston and Austin. Lyle Lovett and Nanci Griffith were playing at Anderson
Fair around the same time. It had two-dollar spaghetti din-
ners every Sunday night and I'd play a set of songs and they'd
let me have my dinner for free. I was playing for my supper.

Hobart was from the Houston area. He had recently finished college at Brown University in Rhode Island and he'd
moved back home to work as a journalist for *The Houston
Chronicle*. His family was one of the few black families in the

South that were able to keep the land they farmed over generations. At some point oil was discovered on the land they owned around Houston and they became very well off. Hobart's grandfather passed the land down to his father, and then, when his father died in 1981, Hobart inherited a lot of money.

Hobart loved music and he came to most of my sets at Anderson Fair. Along with another musician named Bill Priest, we were like the Three Musketeers, running around together. It was totally platonic. We did everything together and Bill and I often played back-to-back sets at various venues. A few years later Hobart went to study with my father in Fayetteville and get his MFA in writing, so it was like we were all family.

Hobart supported me and my music at critical times. Years later, when my career took off, I was able to pay him back every dollar.

Among other things that Hobart did for me, he put together the money to fund a demo tape that I recorded in New York City in January 1983. I had made two records for Folkways by this time and I was hoping to parlay those recordings into a bigger, fuller career, one in which I could stop working odd jobs at record stores, bookstores, restaurants, and health food stores. I must have worked at dozens of these places over the years.

Hobart had become good friends with another student at Brown named David Hirshland, who was looking to get into the music management business. He and Hobart formed a sort of partnership in managing my career for a few very important years. Hobart offered to spend twenty-five thousand dollars to make a demo tape that we would then use to try to get me a record deal with a major label. He and David had another friend from Brown, a musician named Brian Cullman, who had become a producer in New York City, so we hired him to produce the demo. We did the recording at Noise NY in the East Village. Twenty-five thousand dollars was serious money and so Brian was able to hire T-Bone Burnett, David Mansfield, and other major musicians to play on my demo. Brian even got Taj Mahal to come over to play on a track. This was my first time in a professional recording studio with full-time professional musicians.

Throughout this period in the early 1980s I was living with a man named Clyde Joseph Woodward III. I had met him on the Houston music scene. Clyde was another one of these poet-on-a-motorcycle-type guys. He was born into a country-club family, but that's not the kind of person he wanted to be. He was a big man and he was super protective of me and that meant something to me at the time. He wasn't a poet, per se, but he loved a lot of poetic things and he was a reader. He wanted to be a musician but he never applied himself enough to pull it off. My friend the writer Margaret Moser, who was also a close friend of Clyde's, once wrote that he was "a cultural chameleon capable of jaw-dropping magic" and I agree with her. He had a sweet charisma that was extremely appealing to me. He could be the life of any party. He was the kind of guy who somehow knew where to find the best crawfish dives in the smallest towns in Louisiana along with the finest white-tablecloth restaurants in New Orleans while being an expert on the traditional music in that whole region.

Mardi Gras, 1982.

In my song "Lake Charles," named for the small town in Louisiana, which came out on my *Car Wheels* album almost a decade and a half after my relationship with Clyde was over, I wrote these lines about him:

He had a reason to get back to Lake Charles
He used to talk about it

He'd just go on and on
He always said Louisiana
Was where he felt at home.

He was born in Nacogdoches
That's in East Texas
Not far from the border.
But he liked to tell everybody
He was from Lake Charles.

That was Clyde in short. That's the chameleon that Margaret was talking about. He told people he was from a place that he wasn't actually from.

The song continues:

We used to drive
Through Lafayette and Baton Rouge
In a yellow El Camino listening to Howlin' Wolf
He liked to stop in Lake Charles
'Cause that's the place he loves.

Clyde and I would drive all over the area from Houston and Austin to New Orleans and everywhere in between. It was my first relatively long-term relationship. We'd go dancing with Margaret and other friends. In the winter of 1982 we went to the memorial service of Lightnin' Hopkins, one of the greatest blues musicians of all time. A wreath in the shape of a guitar was hung up to honor him, and people were lined up around the block to pay their respects. Another time we were on the road and had nowhere to sleep and we ended up spending the night at Johnny Winter's place. I remember talking to him about Robert Johnson.

Playing at the New Orleans Jazz & Heritage Festival.

Clyde was so much fun to be around but had another side to him that I honestly did not see clearly enough, or did not want to see, during our relationship. He was an alcoholic and over our years together his marijuana addiction morphed into addictions to cocaine and other amphetamines. He had that cycle of death, mixing the depressant of alcohol with the amphetamines. Some of my friends have told me later that he was also dealing drugs but somehow he kept that mostly hidden from me. Clyde loved and worshipped me and despite all his flaws I felt that warmth from him even when he was fucking himself—and us—up.

While we were making the demo tape in New York, Clyde and I stayed in the legendary Chelsea Hotel for several weeks. Hobart's twenty-five thousand dollars of support made that possible. It was the dead of a bitter-cold winter. Each time we left the Chelsea, we'd be freezing—the Chelsea wasn't the best-heated and best-insulated place in the world—so often we ate our meals downstairs in the El Quijote restaurant.

The New York demos have a handful of songs that I'm proud of. I still have the masters. Some of the songs are "Pancakes" and "Jazz Side of Life," which I recorded under a different title for my *Ghosts of Highway 20* record in 2015. But those demos didn't go anywhere. David Hirshland and Brian Cullman did their best to present them to labels. We had meetings and we did showcase performances, but nothing happened. The results were always the same. "We don't

With Clyde in New York City.

know what to do with this," record company executives would say. "It's too country for rock and it's too rock for country." I was stuck in that place between country and rock for two decades.

When I was doing research for this book, I reached out to David and Brian and Hobart for their recollections about this time and they remembered Clyde having a negative, distracting impact on those sessions. He was trying to be protective of me, trying to be my de facto manager, but to them he was just a clumsy bully. Brian even said he was scared of Clyde. I wasn't at all aware of this dynamic. Brian also said it was obvious to him that Clyde was doing a lot of cocaine and it made his moods erratic. I couldn't see that until later.

I knew I had to end the relationship with Clyde a little while later when we were staying at a motel and the phone rang. I picked it up and before I even said anything a man on the other end growled, "Where's my money? Where's my fucking money?" It turns out the guy had given Clyde a bunch of pot to sell and he was looking for his money. I thought, "Fuck, they are going to come after us. We're outlaws."

Digging through the old memories today puts me on a roller coaster of mixed emotions, relishing the victories and reflecting on the imperfections and mistakes. In the end I try to avoid the second-guessing. I think a lot of my decisions back then were fear based. I was afraid to get out of my comfort zone. I had to grow through different levels of my work. I lived and learned. People often assume that I would be bitter that I didn't hit it big until I was well into my forties, but that's not how I feel. It happened when it was meant to happen.

Musically, I was far ahead of where people thought I was. I had a vision and I just had to wait to find a way to fulfill it. The trouble for me was I didn't always know how to communicate my vision, didn't know how to articulate it. I thought about musicians like Lou Reed and the Velvet Underground, and Dylan when he went electric. I wanted to rock way before I was able to. By default I played guitar and sang songs and so I got categorized right off the bat. "You're this cute girl singing folk songs and country songs, so you're a singer-songwriter." It's true I started out with that kind of music, and it was a great background for me, but I aspired to be a literary rock artist. When I heard Chrissie Hynde and the Pretenders' first album in 1980, I thought, "That's it. This is it. This is what I want to do." But I had trouble communicating what I felt and heard in my head.

It took me a long time to get to where I am now. I'm a complete anomaly in the music world, a late bloomer. I believed in myself and I worked very hard and I didn't give up. I also grew up in a family where there wasn't ageism or sexism. The fact that I was still working at taco joints and record stores well into my thirties didn't bother me at all. My parents had flaws but they allowed me to persevere and grow. I grew up believing I could do anything if I was determined enough, even though I didn't even have a high school degree. This came from my father, who really hustled his way into his career, and it also came from my mother, who went right up to John Ciardi and introduced my father to him at that event in Baton Rouge. I think I was born with a certain kind of resilience, or you could call it rebellious attitude. "Nobody's ever going to control me" was my mantra. And I see that thread from my father's father down to my father and to me. I come from a long line of people who are empathetic and who stand up for their own rights and other people's rights. My father and my grandfather had principles that they never let down, and I'm that same girl who grew up under their influence. I haven't changed.

After we finished the New York demos, Clyde and I went back to Texas and I started to be able to see that I needed to be somewhere else and not with him. It was painful because a big part of me really loved Clyde. He did the best he could do. Several months after it became clear that the New York demos weren't helping me get anywhere, David Hirshland came to visit me in Austin. He was living in San Francisco and trying to manage me from there. He told me that I was only going to go so far if I stayed in Texas. I was already feeling that way but it was interesting to hear it from his perspective. I began to work toward moving to Los Angeles. And I had to break up with Clyde.

I moved to Los Angeles in the middle of 1984. Clyde's condition worsened as the years passed and in 1991 I got word that he was in the hospital dying of cirrhosis of the liver. I immediately jumped on a plane at LAX heading to Texas. I wanted to be with Clyde before he died. But when my plane landed, I called the hospital and learned that he'd passed away during my flight. Margaret Moser spent Clyde's final hours and days with him, playing him music that he loved and reading articles to him about subjects that he loved. My song about Clyde, "Lake Charles," has a refrain with these lines that evoke those last hours with Margaret:

> Did an angel whisper in your ear
> And hold you close and take away your fear
> In those long last moments.

11

Hobart and David helped me get an apartment in the Silver Lake neighborhood of L.A. It was a duplex on the southeast corner of Glendale Boulevard and Loma Vista Place for four hundred dollars a month. I had the upstairs and a woman named Mahalia had the downstairs. The songs I wrote in that apartment over the next few years would become some of my most famous.

It was a sweet little one-bedroom apartment that had a room where I set up a desk and where I could sit and look out the back window and see avocado trees in the backyard. I was inspired by this new environment, which was different from anything I was used to. I loved being in new places and that's still true to this day. I know I got this from the nomadic professional life that my father led until I was eighteen years old, when he got the permanent tenured job in Fayetteville. I'm always looking for an excuse to move. I don't like feeling stuck in one place. As soon as I start feeling stuck, I'm outta there.

Even though I loved being in this new apartment in L.A., as usual nothing ever happened easily or quickly. I can't remember all the odd jobs I worked in L.A. over those years to support myself while I played as many shows as I could. Hobart recently reminded me that I worked at a place called Tommy's Tacos, which I had forgotten about. I was a bus girl there. I remember working at Rockaway Records, a great record store in Silver Lake, and Moby Disc, another good one in Sherman Oaks.

Rockaway was a groovy store run by a radical lefty hippie-biker guy named Marty. He refused to stock Steve Earle's album *Guitar Town,* because one of the songs alluded to a "Jap guitar." Marty was such a lefty he wouldn't even stock a record that became a breakthrough for Steve.

I also worked at Pecos Bill's Bar-B-Q stand and I think I worked at Barnes & Noble, but it might have been another one of the chain bookstores. I felt at home in bookstores and record stores. One unusual job I had was selling gourmet sausages at supermarkets. I had a cart that I would set up inside a supermarket and I'd peddle these fine sausages to customers. I cooked samples and offered them on toothpicks. There were different flavors like apple and maple. I loved that job. I made seventy-five dollars for the afternoon and nobody bothered me.

One day I was sitting in the kitchen of my Silver Lake apartment and the phone rang. It was my friend the music journalist John T. Davis, who was also a native Texan. Why do I mention that he is a native Texan? Because Texans, as a rule, don't bullshit you. John T. told me that he had recently gotten a call from someone who was a fan of mine who loved my Folkways records. He told John that he recognized one of my songs in a porn film called *All American Girls in Heat*. This is when the old Alpha Music contract came back to haunt me. I didn't have any control over those songs. I just about fell out of my chair onto the kitchen floor. I didn't know whether to laugh or cry. I hadn't read between the lines of the Alpha contract and I didn't have an attorney to help me back then.

I told my manager about this and he made a call to my attorney, Rosemary Carroll. She called Mike Nurko, the head of Alpha, and he had nothing much to say. He said there was no money involved, my little innocent song was exchanged, and now I was part of an X-rated porn film. My manager, in the interest of detective work, went out and found a copy of the film and rented it. He viewed it and then told me the plot. Again, I didn't know whether to laugh or cry.

I saw the film at some point later. It was no big deal, really. There's a rusty old gas station out west with an old school bus parked outside. A couple of lanky cowboys are standing around a pickup truck at the gas pump. A pretty young girl in a miniskirt saunters out of the school bus—the insinuation is that she's a student. She makes her way over to the cowboys and she has one line. One line! "You boys got anything I can fill up with?" The cowboys feign surprise. The girl wanders over to them. What happens next is not original. They start going at it in the back of the truck, inside the cab, and outside the truck on the dusty dirty ground. I can't remember exactly when my song can be heard.

In L.A., I was playing as many live sets as I could. I would play anywhere—coffeehouses, bars and taverns, clubs of all kinds. I had an old Saab that I would drive all over Los Angeles County, sometimes to play a set that lasted only thirty minutes.

One of the great things about L.A. in the 1980s was that the music scene was wide open in terms of genre. I felt liberated from the singer-songwriter and cosmic cowboy scene in Texas. Today you can get a glimpse of my early days in L.A. by looking through old issues of the *LA Weekly* where you can find my name on the same weekly bill with bands like Jane's Addiction and X and the Long Ryders and the Blasters at clubs like Raji's and the Troubadour and McCabe's and Club Lingerie and the Palomino. That never would have happened in Texas. In L.A. nobody asked or cared what

genre you were in, at least not the club managers or the listeners. The record labels, as always, though, were a bit slow
to embrace what was happening underground.

Playing at nightclubs in L.A.

Dirty garage music mixed with country music in L.A.; as
far as I know, that was the only place where that mix was
happening. The scene was equal parts X, the Germs, the
Blasters, the Ramones, Los Lobos, and Merle Haggard.
L.A. was the beginning of what became known as "alterna-
tive country," which is a term I actually hate. I know that
today I'm often seen as one of the pioneers of alt-country
and "Americana" and I accept that as an intended compliment, but I resist those terms because they're just more

genres or categories that people—people at record companies, mostly—need and cling to for various reasons, mostly commercial ones.

Sometimes this mixed-genre scene in L.A. is called the Paisley Underground and that's another one of those terms that I try to resist. One of the groups that perfectly exemplified this blend of styles was the Long Ryders. They were a great country rock punk band. At some point in late 1984 or 1985, I started opening shows for them. One night at Raji's there was a drunk man in the audience heckling me. In between songs he'd yell out, "You need the Long Ryders, you couldn't do it on your own, you aren't anything without the Long Ryders." Well, the guys in the Long Ryders didn't like that, so a barroom brawl broke out and this heckler ended up in the hospital. An LAPD detective called and said that the man was going to press charges against the guys in the band unless they let him open a few shows. It turned out he was a disgruntled musician.

I began dating the drummer in the Long Ryders, Greg Sowders. We had met at the Music Machine. I was playing a benefit show with Dave Alvin and others. Greg was a skinny guy, cute, had long hair, a cowboy hat, a nice smile, a sparkle in his eyes, and he charmed his way into my life. He used to tell me, "I'm your ace in the hole." He also had some of that bad boy in him.

Greg moved in with me in the duplex in Silver Lake and eventually we got married. But the relationship wasn't meant to last. He was seven years younger than me, which is neither

With my first husband, Greg, at our wedding.

here nor there. The main problem was that we were both working all the time and he was on the road a lot with the band, and we never really had a chance to work on our relationship. We divorced after just a year and a half. I'm still friends with him and his second wife today. When my husband, Tom, and I got married in 2009, they came to our wedding.

Even though our marriage didn't last, the time Greg and I shared together was extremely productive for me professionally. That's when I wrote the songs that ended up on my

1988 self-titled album for Rough Trade Records. Greg says that I wrote all of my best songs during periods that were dark for me, emotionally and psychologically, when I was depressed and anxious and when my obsessive-compulsive disorder was heightened. I don't quite remember it that way, but I'm sure his observations are valid. I do believe that music was my therapy for dealing with many of the traumas I suffered as a child, beginning when I got my guitar at age twelve, and probably still today at age seventy. In general, though, I don't believe my periodic depression is helpful to my songwriting or anything else in my life. I realize, to be honest, that my unpredictable moods have caused some problems for others at times, when people are expecting me to do this or that and I do something else instead. I've battled something resembling an obsessive-compulsive disorder that often rears its head when I'm beginning to feel depressed. It's as if the OCD is a way of coping. As if there's something I'm supposed to be doing and I'll decide to rearrange everything in my closets instead of doing that thing while people are waiting for me.

Several things happened in L.A. that propelled me forward. One was that David and Hobart had done a great job of packaging me and marketing me to venues. In the fall of 1985, I was part of a series of shows called "Millions of Williams" that included Victoria Williams and the Williams Brothers, who were nephews of the famous singer Andy Williams. Then for almost a year I had what was called a residency at Al's Bar, a great club in an abandoned hotel in downtown L.A. I played there every week for months with David Mansfield on guitar and David Miner on bass. They were both in T-Bone Burnett's Alpha Band. Mansfield, of course, was part of Dylan's Rolling Thunder Revue and he'd played on my New York demos a couple of years earlier. He was now living in L.A. David, David, and I were a great trio with no drummer. I wish we had recorded.

LA Weekly described Al's Bar perfectly in its listings: "The famous downtown bastion for bohemian barflies is again offering varied entertainment. Located in the midst of the burgeoning loft neighborhood, this comfortable hangout would make Edward Hopper and Charles Bukowski proud and features one of the best jukeboxes in the city, with selections running the gamut from Hank Williams to Echo and the Bunnymen."

I love the literary reference to a writer I actually knew from my father's parties back in Fayetteville. Al's Bar kind of summed up what I was trying to do. *LA Weekly* was also very supportive of me, often touting my shows. People were taking notice of what I was doing.

Raji's is another place that was very important to me. It was a funky spot in Hollywood. *LA Weekly* described it well, too: "If you crossed the Ramones with the Arabian Nights you might come up with something close to this club. His sultanic majesty Dobbs serves the beer and wine cold, the Mexican food hot, and the rock and roll nonstop."

One time a few executives from Rounder Records in New York flew out to L.A. to see me play at Raji's. I didn't have my own band yet, but members of the Long Ryders sat in for me. Everybody was drinking and having a good time. I thought things were going well. But then the next day I met with the executives and they told me, "We like you, but we just don't think you're ready to take a band on the road. Your show isn't polished enough." Something similar happened with Rhino Records and Hightone Records and others.

Right around that time I had another gig at Raji's with the musicians who would later become my full-time band— Gurf Morlix on guitar, John Ciambotti on bass, and Donald Lindley on drums. The club gave us five one-dollar bills for the show, so I could give each of the guys one dollar and I kept two. For some reason, those guys decided to hang in there with me. I think they could feel that something was going to happen.

Shortly after that I got the break I needed. Columbia Records offered me a development deal in the amount of thirty-five thousand dollars. Ron Oberman called me into his office at Columbia in Beverly Hills and told me he really liked me and believed in me. The agreement he offered was that the advance would go toward living expenses for six months while I recorded a demo with a band. The label would review the demo and decide whether to give me a full record deal.

I remember driving back to Silver Lake from Beverly Hills and thinking, "Wow, this is fucking amazing. Somebody's giving me a real chance." I was over the moon.

The Columbia deal bought me a lot of time to finish songs I'd started writing years earlier, and to write new songs. I was able to quit the odd jobs and focus on the music. I would wake up in my Silver Lake duplex and sit out in the morning sun on the back balcony and write. Then, in the afternoon, when the sun was coming through the west-facing windows, I'd sit in the living room and write songs. And then Gurf, John, Donald, and I would play those songs in shows at night.

I wrote "Changed the Locks" during that time in Silver Lake. It's a classic blues with lyrics about unrequited love, which was a subject I knew well. Those are the easiest songs to write, especially when you are young and going through turbulence in all sorts of different relationships. Same thing with "Abandoned," which I wrote in Silver Lake. Neither of those songs is about anyone in particular, just the ending of relationships in general.

I also wrote "Crescent City" there. That song contains so many little documentary pieces from my life. There is a connection with Clyde because he loved Louisiana and New Orleans and reveling, drinking, and dancing with friends. My brother's in that song, and my sister and my mother. Mandeville is a mental hospital named after a small town of the same name on the outskirts of New Orleans. My mother spent some time there during one of her tough periods. At this time, I stayed in closer touch with my father because I would send him song lyrics to read and give me feedback (he was a poet, after all), but I never stopped thinking about my brother and sister and of course my mother. "Crescent City" is a compact song filled with autobiographical connections to them.

One of my favorite songs of my career was written there, "Side of the Road." I had a tendency to lose myself in relationships and I was thinking about that a lot. Many women will give themselves over to men and completely lose any sense of who they are as individuals. I did that time after time. I became like a bird in a cage that had to get out. This is how I felt about my marriage to Greg, even though I know it was as much my fault as his. I'd been doing therapy to try to avoid losing myself in these men. I was also inspired by a painting by Andrew Wyeth that I'd seen in a book a few years earlier. It was a picture of a lonely woman.

"Passionate Kisses" is about Greg. The Long Ryders were taking off and he was on the road constantly in the States and over in Europe. This was the first time I was with somebody who was always gone. Usually I was the one who was always out or gone. The song, musically, owes a lot to Joan Armatrading. "Am I Too Blue" and "Big Red Sun Blues" are also about Greg. Even though our relationship was structurally fraught because we were two full-time musicians trying to make careers happen, I tended to blame my own depression or blues for the problems.

I had begun writing "I Just Wanted to See You So Bad" in 1979 or 1980 but I didn't finish it until I landed the Columbia deal. It's about a poet I had a deep crush on, Bruce Weigl. I had been living in Houston at the time and I had a gig in

Little Rock and Bruce had a poetry reading there at the same time. I don't remember how we actually met. Maybe he'd known my dad through the poetry world. In any case, I was immediately smitten. I attended his reading and he attended my show. He had that quality that I've mentioned—the rugged, good-looking poet, like Sam Shepard—handsome, funny, brilliant, and rough and tumble. The sensitive masculine guy. There's part of me that wants to stay up all night and talk about philosophy and art and there's another part of me that wants to be dragged into the bedroom. Bruce was another one of these guys who could do both.

After Little Rock, Bruce and I kept in touch. Then one day I was at home in Houston when I got a call from him. He told me he was in San Antonio for a writers' conference, and did I want to come over for the weekend? Of course I said yes and threw some things in a bag, jumped in my Saab, and drove to San Antonio. His conference was in a beautiful Art Deco hotel downtown by the river. As I was driving to San Antonio, I had no idea what was going to happen. I thought we were going to have this wonderful weekend love affair.

Of course it didn't end well. When I arrived, Bruce thought it was a good time to let me know that he was married and his wife was pregnant. So much for that. But the feelings I had for Bruce and the anticipation of that meeting in San Antonio helped me create a song that opened an album that changed my life.

"The Night's Too Long" was done before the Columbia

deal. I wrote it not long after I moved to L.A. I like to think of that song as being inspired by the movie *Looking for Mr. Goodbar,* but it was also about going out at night and seeing some of the same women repeatedly. I went out a lot in those days. I was young and single, and as a musician that's what you did, you went to check out other musicians. There are certain people you see around a lot of different bands. Maybe I was one of them. So there was a little bit of myself in that song, too. As a writer you have to be empathetic toward the people you're writing about. Sylvia was a young woman running away to start a new life. That's not unlike what I had done several times. Sylvia left a small town to go to a big city because she was bored and tired of these small-town people and she wanted to find a guy who wore a leather jacket. That could have been me driving from Austin to Los Angeles, and Greg the guy in the leather jacket.

These were the songs I was preparing to record for the demo. They were also the songs that I was playing in shows at the same time. Columbia brought in Henry Lewy to produce my demo. He was a big deal. He'd produced all of Joni Mitchell's breakthrough records, including *Blue,* and he also produced records with Neil Young and Leonard Cohen. Henry brought in a number of famous musicians to play on my demo—Garth Hudson from the Band, Terry Adams from NRBQ, and the legendary New Orleans pianist Henry Butler. I was flattered and hopeful having these famous musicians playing my music, but looking back, we probably should have cut the demo with my regular band instead of this all-star crew. Ron Oberman and his colleagues in the L.A. offices of Columbia listened to the resulting demo and declined to offer me a full record deal. They said it was too country for rock. They sent the tape to the Columbia executives in Nashville, who said it was too rock for country.

Even though I was extremely deflated, I managed to summon the energy, with the help and affirmation from David and Hobart, to go through another series of meetings and showcases with labels, using the new demo. Every single one of them passed on me. The big labels, the small labels, we tried them all and they all passed on me, most of them for the second time.

I was tired of all the label guys—and they were all guys—sniffing around me and saying I was really good and unique and original and getting my hopes up and then backing away at the last minute. One of the label guys, Peter Philbin at Elektra, kept coming to my shows and then he called me in for another meeting during which he told me, "I don't think your songs are really finished. They don't have proper bridges. You have a uniquely beautiful voice, but as far as songwriting and song structure you need to go back to the drawing board." One of the songs Philbin used as an example was "Changed the Locks." "What kind of song is this?" he asked me. "There's no bridge in it. This isn't a finished song."

We'd met at my apartment in Silver Lake. After he left, I got out my Neil Young and Bob Dylan albums to remind myself that it was okay that my songs didn't have bridges.

More than three decades later, "Changed the Locks" remains one of my most popular songs, and its structure is the same as it was then. In 1996, it was covered beautifully by Tom Petty, one of my favorite songwriters and artists. Now, that's something to be proud of.

12

One thing I learned over the years is that if you put in hard work, it will get rewarded in some manner. It could be an indirect reward and it might not happen as fast as you want it to, but your efforts of passion and determination always matter.

I didn't know this in 1986, though, so I was depressed by being rejected by every label after having recorded a significant demo. I considered moving back to Texas. To be honest, one reason I hadn't moved back already was that so many of my friends in Texas had scoffed at my original decision to move to L.A. There's a particular provincial quality to Texas, a feeling that you have everything you need there, that there's no reason to go anywhere else. In a way it reminds me of the way some New Yorkers are about New York City. Not all Texans and not all New Yorkers, but a lot of them. A few people in Texas actually told me when they learned I was moving to L.A., "We'll see you back here in six months or a year." That sticks in my craw still today.

The reality was that I was now thirty-three years old, which back then was ancient for a relatively unknown female singer. It might still be ancient now. I had spent two full years in L.A. playing every show at every venue that would have me, and for most of that time I was also working at energy-zapping day jobs in order to pay bills, and now I was back working at those jobs again. I was exhausted and demoralized, but I kept at it. I still believed. Gurf, Donald, John, and I kept playing shows with the repertoire I had developed. They still believed, too.

Around that time I recorded a song for a compilation album called *A Town South of Bakersfield*. During that recording I worked with the engineer Dusty Wakeman, who would become a lifelong friend. Dusty connected me with Pete Anderson, who was a big name around L.A. at that time, playing with and producing Dwight Yoakam. Pete liked my music and wanted to help me get a record deal. He got a band together and I recorded yet another demo with him, this one with just four songs on it. When it was all said and done, I wasn't happy with it. I called Pete and said, "I don't like this." I told him it was overproduced and it didn't represent what I wanted it to at all. He responded something to the effect of

"That doesn't really matter. We just need to get our foot in the door and then we can do whatever we want." I replied that my instincts told me that wasn't going to happen and I wouldn't be happy with the results even if it did. I had this innate fear of being overproduced, too slick. None of the records I revered were overproduced and slick. I worried that record people would hear this new demo and think that this was the kind of record I wanted to make.

Pete paused on the phone and then he said, "You're right. It sucks. And it's too wet," meaning that it had too much reverb on it.

Nothing happened to that tape, either. In so many words, I had told one of the most respected producers in L.A. that he didn't know what he was doing.

I was back working at a record store and selling sausages in supermarkets. All the decision-making people in the music industry were men. So come to think of it, I was pitching sausages on two different levels.

One day, when things seemed most dire and I was sitting around the Silver Lake apartment, Greg was on the road with the Long Ryders, and nothing was happening in my career except the same shows around L.A., my phone rang and it was a man named Robin Hurley from Rough Trade Records, the British punk label that had recently, unbeknownst to me, opened an office in San Francisco called Rough Trade

America. Copies of my Columbia demo tape had been floating around and occasionally college radio stations or independent radio stations would play tracks from it. I don't know how Robin learned about it, but he got his hands on that Columbia demo. He also found his way to my Folkways record *Happy Woman Blues,* which he loved. He told me, "We love your voice and we love your songs. Do you want to make a record with Rough Trade?"

I almost fell on the floor. From my experience it took extraordinary balls for an executive to just flatly say the things that Robin said. No meetings, no showcases, no discussions of this or that, no bullshit, just flat out directly saying we love this and we want to make your record. "I'm in," I said.

I've always enjoyed saying that it took a British punk label to give me a chance to make a commercial record. Something about that was perfect. I later learned that when Robin took his job at Rough Trade America, his charge was to find vital and unknown American musicians, ones that didn't fit into molds created by commercial bureaucrats. Robin sent the Columbia demo over to Geoff Travis, the overall head of Rough Trade in the U.K. Geoff had signed artists like the Smiths and Aztec Camera. Robin didn't think Geoff would like my demo but he actually loved it as much as Robin did.

This was a no-brainer for me. Rough Trade was a great, iconoclastic label, the kind of outlier place where I needed to be. They offered me a budget of fifteen thousand dollars to make the record, which was less than what Hobart had fronted me for the New York demos. But that didn't matter to me. This was a real label with character and vision and courage.

One of the benefits of working with a lower studio budget was that we just had to go in there and do it. No fucking around. When I first got the deal, Gurf and I brainstormed different producers to approach, but we didn't have the budget, which ended up being a blessing. One day a friend said to me, "Why don't you and Gurf just produce it yourselves?" Yeah, I thought, we can do this.

Gurf was originally from Buffalo but he had moved to Texas in his twenties, and when I first met him, he was playing with Blaze Foley. I liked him from the start, but we didn't become committed collaborators until we were both living in L.A. A slender man with long dark hair parted down the middle, he had a natural way with the guitar and he didn't overplay his solos, which I admired.

The band and I already had the songs ready from playing them so many times in shows. We could go into the studio and play the songs like we had played them live. That's probably how most of the punk bands on Rough Trade did it. We'll do that, I thought. And we did. We recorded the record in Dusty Wakeman's studio, Mad Dog, in Venice Beach in June 1988. At most, we spent a couple of weeks and the record was done. I think we did basically one song a day. It was a very organic approach that I still prefer today.

The record came out later in 1988 and my life changed. I was ready for it. I was thirty-five years old and basically had been playing music every day since I was twelve, hustling day jobs to make ends meet. Rough Trade sent me to Europe and around the States. It was the first time I was able to say to myself, "Wow, I'm doing this. I'm playing music and singing for a living. It's working." And I've been able to do that ever since.

Sometimes I think back to that little duplex apartment in Silver Lake where most of the Rough Trade songs were written, when I really didn't know how things were going to work out. I have this one distinct memory of leaving the apartment in the dark and going for a walk in Silver Lake one night, or it might have been early morning before the sun came up. I wandered all through the neighborhood and ended up at a vista that overlooked a baseball field and for some reason the lights were on even though there wasn't a game or anything happening. There were no people there, but the field was lit up. There was a small pack of coyotes wandering around the ball field. I stood there and watched them from a distance. The field must have been watered regularly to keep the grass alive, so I'm guessing the coyotes would go there and lick water off the grass. I just stood there and watched.

13

The success of the Rough Trade record created new kinds of pressures that I'd never felt before. The pressure now was not so much about how to make a living as what am I going to do next? Everybody would ask me, what are you working on now? I didn't like that feeling too much, that I now had to measure up to a standard that I had set. I knew I had to write good new songs, songs as good as the ones on that record. But I'd had my entire life to write those songs. Some of those songs had been simmering in my head for years before I ever started playing them or writing them down.

Now all of the major labels that had turned me down for years were coming back around and trying to sign me.

They wanted me now, but I didn't want to sign with a big label. Fuck the big labels. I wanted to stay with Rough Trade because they were so supportive of me when nobody else was and it felt like a little family there. But I was already learning that they had limited resources. Record stores would only order a certain number of Rough Trade albums. They didn't have the promotion and distribution reach of a bigger label.

Then I got this offer from Bob Buziak at RCA. The only reason I considered it was that Bob was cool and he had a good reputation. He had signed a lot of great, edgy artists like the Cowboy Junkies and Treat Her Right, whose lead singer went on to start the band Morphine. I was ignorant and naïve enough to think that Rough Trade and RCA could collaborate, that it could be Rough Trade/RCA. I decided to sign with RCA and it was a brutal decision that I later came to regret. Rough Trade tried to sue me for breach of contract, but my lawyer realized that they had let the recording agreement expire and I was free to go. I stayed friendly with Robin Hurley, and when we produced the twenty-fifth anniversary edition of that album, I asked him to write an essay for the liner notes and he wrote something beautiful.

Almost as soon as I signed with RCA, Bob Buziak left for a similar job at Elektra Records. I didn't blame Bob for leaving and I later came to understand why he left; he was mired in a stifling corporate bureaucracy. So here I was contractually stuck with RCA without the whole reason—Bob—that I had considered signing there in the first place. The new guy that came in to replace Bob had just transferred from Nashville. I don't remember his name but everybody said he was "a numbers man."

I'll never forget something that happened when Gurf, John, Donald, and I started production rehearsals for the next album. A man named Bennett Kaufman was assigned to be my A&R (artist and repertoire) person at the label and he came to the rehearsal room in L.A. to talk about possible producers for the album. I threw out the name Bob Johnston. Kaufman goes, "Who is Bob Johnston?" I said, "He produced *Blonde on Blonde*." Kaufman said, "What's *Blonde on Blonde*? Is that a new band?"

His credibility was shot with me. He had never heard of one of the greatest albums of all time. I remember thinking, "This is really fucked. These people don't have a clue." I was miserable. People were getting kicked off labels left and right in those days but I couldn't get myself kicked off RCA. I was saying to them, "Please let me go." But they wouldn't let me go.

Despite those feelings of doom, the band and I trudged forward and we started recording songs. The process was almost the opposite of the organic process we used to make the Rough Trade record. We didn't have to rehearse those songs, because we'd been playing them in shows. With the new record, we had to rehearse new songs, plus we had goofballs looking over our shoulders.

RCA wanted "Six Blocks Away" to be the first single, so we started working on that one first. We got an initial mix of the song done and the L.A. people at RCA sent it to their New York offices for Dave Thoener to do a remix for the radio. I had never dealt with this kind of process before. This was back before digital recordings, so when they sent the rough mix to New York, it was a hard-copy tape sent by FedEx or UPS or whatever. It felt as if something very precious were being let go and sent to some unknown place where strangers were going to mess with it. This actually felt worse than the guys looking over our shoulders.

One day Kaufman called me from his office in Beverly Hills and said, "Hey, I got the remixed track back from New York. Come over to my office and we'll listen to it." So I drove over to Beverly Hills and at this point I had a major attitude working. I walked into Kaufman's office and he played the track and he jumped up and down in his Gucci shoes and said, "Isn't this great? It sounds like a record now. It sounds like a real record," like it hadn't sounded like a real record until Thoener got his slick hands on it. He had pushed the bass and drums way up to the front and my vocal back, which was a standard pop mixing style in the early 1990s. To be fair, Thoener probably did this only because he was hired to do it that way.

"I fucking hate this," I said. "I hate it." Even though I told them that, they went ahead and tried to put this remix out as a single. I fought them tooth and nail every step of the way. I was right. It sounded awful.

During this time, I was invited to South by Southwest in Austin to take part in a public panel discussion called "How

Does Commercialism Affect Creativity?" Oh, man. This was perfect. Now I had a forum for my story.

When it was my turn to talk in Austin, I laid it all out exactly as it had happened at RCA. I was bluntly honest. The next day I got a call from my manager, who was livid. He worked for one of the biggest promoters in the business. He said, "Congratulations, you got kicked off RCA." He was unhappy about it, but I was exuberant. I was free. I ended up signing with Bob Buziak again, this time at Chameleon, a division of Elektra Records, where he was now working.

My brother, Robert, as a teenager.

One of the songs I wrote during this period, "Little Angel, Little Brother," remains one of my favorites, maybe the best song I've ever written. It's a melancholy homage to my brother, Robert, who is two years younger than me. It's a list of images and impressions I had of my brilliant little brother, with a touch of sorrow. He read all of Shakespeare and he memorized much of it. He had the potential to be a great musician. He was so talented. After high school he lived most of the time in New Orleans, where my mother was living, and at one point he had a one-man musical act and his stage name was Rockin' Bob. He played piano and sang really well. But there would be long periods when I wouldn't know where he was. One time when I was still married to Greg, the Long Ryders had shows in New Orleans and Greg spent some time trying to find Robert without any luck. Sometimes he could be found at my mother's apartment. He would show up there and play her piano for hours on end and stay for days or weeks or months at a time. Then he would disappear for a while and come back. Something had happened to him that I still don't understand to this day. I can only speak to the traumas and struggles of my childhood; I'm not sure what Robert's struggles were.

I have a vivid memory of visiting my mother in New Orleans once at Christmastime and I walked in from outside and a figure appeared in the hallway. It was Mama in her nightgown. I could smell the alcohol coming through her pores. She motioned to me, as if signaling something. She managed a half smile. I waved back. She wanted me to know that she was there. Robert was in the kitchen. He and I left and went to a bar. We talked about music and other things. We didn't discuss what was going on with our mother. We didn't really need to.

Today Robert lives with a friend in Los Angeles almost as a recluse. We're barely in touch. Periodically, I'll send him emails, ask him if he wants to get together, but he rarely responds. One time fairly recently I sent him a note that said nothing but "I love you," and he responded with simply "I love you, too." His response meant so much to me, as if the sky had opened up. But I wish I knew more about him. I wish we were closer.

Your R&B records and your music books
Your sense of humor and your rugged good
    looks

I see you now at the piano
Your back a slow curve
Playing Ray Charles and Fats Domino
While I sang all the words.

Little angel, little brother

Your bad habits and your attitude
Your restless ways and your solitude

I see you leaning your lanky frame
Just inside the door

A figure behind the kitchen screen
Staring down at the floor

Little angel, little brother
Little angel, little brother

Your passion for Shakespeare and your
    paperbacks
Your chess pieces and your wisecracks

I see you sleeping in the car
Curled up on the backseat
Parked outside of a bar
An empty bottle at your feet.

Little angel, little brother.

I love singing that song, but each time I do it I almost cry. Sometimes I do cry.

Sweet Old World was released by Chameleon in 1992. One of the songs that is significant is "Hot Blood" because it was the first time I'd written explicitly about lust, which is one of those things that women aren't supposed to do, even though the history of rock and roll could be told from men writing songs about lust. You could go on and on with examples, like "Brown Sugar" and "Let's Spend the Night Together" by the Stones, "The Lemon Song" by Zeppelin, "Foxey Lady" by Hendrix, "Light My Fire" by the Doors, "Sexual Healing" by

Marvin Gaye, and almost everything James Brown ever did, to name just a few.

"Hot Blood" wasn't based on anybody in particular. I imagined a woman character for the point of view in that song, although like all the characters I imagine there's a little of me in there.

By this time I had relocated to Nashville. Steve Earle and Emmylou Harris and Rosanne Cash were living there at that time. John Prine was there. Nanci Griffith. I knew a lot of these musicians personally by then. It felt like a good place for me to be. Greg and I had already split, so it was the right time to make a move.

But I didn't have a very good attitude when I first landed in Nashville. I hated what had happened to country music. I had trouble with the idea of two, three, four, or even five or six people writing a song together. I didn't like the sound of the current country music at the time, the slick way it was being produced. It didn't help that shortly after I arrived in town, I was asked to be on the TV show *Crook & Chase,* an early morning coffee-and-breakfast show. I agreed. It would be good exposure, I thought. I told the producers I wanted to perform my song "Pineola" and they bristled. It was too dark, they said. It wasn't "good morning music," they said. It didn't fit their idea of wholesome American morning music. But it was the only song I wanted to sing on their show, so I stuck to my guns. Finally, they relented, but it left a bad taste in my mouth. It pushed my rebel buttons. I sensed that Nashville wasn't going to work out for me.

Later the same year something really good happened. Mary Chapin Carpenter covered "Passionate Kisses" and it went to the top of the charts, exposing my music to a whole different world of popular music fans. I won a Grammy for Best Country Song for that song. My reaction was mixed. Of course, I was honored and excited and I felt much gratitude to Carpenter for giving me this kind of exposure, but I was also insecure and terrified. The thought of actually attending the Grammy ceremony, for example, was overwhelmingly frightening. My mind was racing: "What am I going to wear? Will I look good? Are my teeth pretty enough?" I was looking at myself through a microscope.

Rosanne Cash told me about a shop in New York where they would treat me right and fit me with a nice outfit for the Grammys. I was now forty-one years old and making enough money that I could afford to do something like that. But my mindset was still that of the girl working in the record store or taco stand or selling sausages in the supermarket.

My trip to New York was all set up. I had a flight booked, I had a hotel room, and Rosanne arranged an appointment at the clothing shop and they knew my sizes and everything and they had selections of outfits waiting for me to try on. That afternoon my friend Dub was going to pick me up and take me to the airport in Nashville. When he arrived, I was still in my pajamas and I hadn't packed my bag or anything. "Lu, what in the hell are you doing?" he asked.

"Let's go down to the Sunset Grill and get something to eat and have a glass of wine," I said.

I didn't go to New York. I didn't go to the Grammys. I froze in fear. Afterward, when the story of my decision emerged, people asked, "You get up and play in front of all those people all the time . . . what was the problem?"

"I know, I know," I would say. "I just get self-conscious in front of certain kinds of people."

The truth is that I was not just self-conscious but also scared. I feared that I didn't belong. It's a feeling I've been trying to shake my entire life. It's a riddle I believe many artists have been trying to solve for centuries. It takes enormous fortitude to create the work in the first place, but then once it's time to put it out in the world, the confidence required to go public is unrelated to the audacity that created the work. I'm not as stricken by that fear now as I used to be, but it can still pop up from time to time.

14

S*weet Old World* brought me more attention and more opportunities, offers to do shows and festivals around the
world, offers to sing on other people's albums. I spent most
of the next two years on the road. I loved—and still love—
being on the road, living in buses and hotels. I'm at home in
that routine still today.

During that *Sweet Old World* tour I developed a relationship with Roly Salley, who was in my band at the time. He
was the longtime bass player in Chris Isaak's band and he
also played with John Prine. He played bass in my band on
the *Sweet Old World* tour. He was another of the funny, intelligent, and enigmatic men who entered my life and ended up

inspiring several songs on my next record, which would be *Car Wheels on a Gravel Road*.

Roly doggedly pursued me and I was immediately smitten with him. We had a very unusual sexual chemistry and got real tangled up with each other. The songs "Joy" and "Still I Long for Your Kiss" are about Roly. I remember Gurf pulling me aside at a bar one night and warning me about Roly. But I completely fell down the rabbit hole anyway. I took the relationship with Roly very seriously and I remember even thinking, "We're going to buy a house together." When I start thinking about getting houses, that's when you know I should be careful.

I was still dating another man, named Lorne, and was committed to him, when Roly started pursuing me. One night we were in New York City and Lorne came to town for the shows. So we were all in the same hotel. I decided I had to be an adult about the situation and tell Lorne about my feelings for Roly. Lorne didn't say a word. He started picking up things in the hotel room—lamps, chairs, tables, the television—and throwing them as hard as he could against the wall. I was sitting on the side of the bed terrified. I was afraid he was going to hurt me, but he never did.

I finally made it out of the hotel room and down to the lobby, where I called my tour manager, who went up to the room to calm Lorne down. A little while later my tour manager told me I could go back to the room. I went up there and Lorne had bought a six-pack of Budweiser and was

sitting on the bed drinking beer. He was alternating between crying and bitching at me. We stayed up all night
talking about it, how this was the end of the relationship.

The next morning I said goodbye to Lorne, bless his
heart, and I walked up the steps onto the tour bus and sat
down next to Roly. You see what's coming now, but I couldn't
see it then. "I broke up with Lorne so I'm free now," I told
Roly. "I'm yours." He immediately had a look on his face that
I had never seen before, like he was shocked and petrified,
like he was thinking, "Oh my God, what the fuck?" Everything between us changed at that moment. At one point he
said, "We have to get off this metal firecracker," which is
what he called the tour bus, "because everything is going to
explode." What he meant was, let's wait until we get the tour
done and then we can continue. Of course, that never happened. Once we got off the metal firecracker our relationship went to shit. He didn't keep his promise. But he kept me
hanging on for a while.

Right after that tour ended, I was at a strawberry festival
in Northern California and I was still really hung up on him.
The festival organizers had put me up in one of these log
cabins that didn't have a phone. There was a phone booth
out in the parking lot. I went into the phone booth and called
Roly and I said, "I'm sick and tired of this bullshit. I need to
know where I stand."

"I love you but this relationship doesn't fit into my agenda
right now," he said.

"Okay," I said, and hung up. I went to my room and cried and cried. I learned later that he was involved with a lot of women at the same time he was with me, some of them famous musicians. I won't name names. That relationship was done, but I got a good song out of it that would be featured on my *Car Wheels* record.

Once we rode together in a metal firecracker
You told me I was your queen
You told me I was your biker
You told me I was everything
Once I was in your blood
And you were obsessed with me
You wanted to paint my picture
You wanted to undress me
You wanted to see me in your future

All I ask, don't tell anybody the secrets
Don't tell anybody the secrets I told you
All I ask, don't tell anybody the secrets
Don't tell anybody the secrets I told you

Once you held me so tight
I thought I'd lose my mind
You said I rocked your world
You said it was for all time
You said that I would always be your girl
We'd put on ZZ Top

Lucinda Williams

And turn 'em up real loud
I used to think you were strong
I used to think you were proud
I used to think nothing could go wrong

All I ask, don't tell anybody the secrets
Don't tell anybody the secrets I told you
All I ask, don't tell anybody the secrets
Don't tell anybody the secrets I told you

15

After the *Sweet Old World* tour I was looking around for a new label. Chameleon and Elektra had folded. I wasn't too worried about it, because people were coming to me with offers.

Around 1995, Rick Rubin started expressing interest in signing me to his label, American Recordings. He wanted to produce my next record. He invited me and my band over to his house in Los Angeles. This was a big deal at the time. Rick had made a name for himself founding Def Jam Recordings with Russell Simmons and working with artists like Public Enemy, LL Cool J, and the Beastie Boys. He was at a point in his career where he could be very careful and selective about who he worked with.

Rick's house was full of religious symbols. He had replicas and statues and paintings of Buddha and Jesus all over the walls. There was Buddha wallpaper and stained-glass windows that he'd had excavated from abandoned churches. At the same time there was an industrial feel to the bathrooms, like you were in a downtown loft in a converted warehouse. Rick was physically impressive, too, a very large man with long wavy hair and a long thick beard and blue eyes. He looked like a walking religious symbol himself.

After we arrived, Rick played us the new PJ Harvey record as an example of a direction he could see me going. I loved that idea. Rick could sense that I wanted to rock out a bit harder. He got me in a way that most other people hadn't yet.

The only problem was that Gurf didn't like the idea. As I was having more success, Gurf started seeing himself as my music director or co-collaborator, like a co-pilot or something. He wanted more and more control over the music, and more credit for it, and he didn't want to work with another producer like Rick.

At the time I felt ready to try some new things as a songwriter. Something was welling up in me but I couldn't put words to it yet. The Rough Trade record and *Sweet Old World* had been successful and I was now in a position to grow and move forward, not concerned so much about gaining a foothold anymore, but ready to actually take steps up the creative ladder. I was in my forties now and I wasn't the girl working retail any longer.

I was living in Nashville in one of those chain hotels that caters to long-term renters, a Stay at Home Suites or Extended Stay or something like that. That's where I wrote a lot of the songs for what became *Car Wheels on a Gravel Road*. I liked the idea of not having a big commitment like a lease or mortgage. It seemed to free up my creativity. I had a pullout Murphy bed and there was a laundry room in the building. Most of the songs I wrote for the record there are about my childhood, my love life, or my career.

Two of the first new songs I wrote were "Lake Charles," about Clyde, and "Drunken Angel," about the musician Blaze Foley, who I had known and befriended when I was living in Texas. Both men were done in by their self-destructive habits.

I started "Lake Charles" in 1992 or 1993 while I was on the road for the *Sweet Old World* tour. Clyde had died in 1991 and I'd had all these ideas in my head about him for a long time. He was one of those people who had more potential than he fulfilled. He was supersmart and really funny and soulful, but he was also fucked up, and he could be abusive. Not physically, to me, but verbally. We had these horrific fights including one I remember when he picked up a plate and smashed it against the wall.

There was one night in 1981 when Blaze Foley was playing at a club and Clyde and I went. Legendary Texas singer-songwriter Butch Hancock was there. Butch and I had this little flirty crush going on between us. It never amounted to anything but Clyde picked up on it. After the show he threatened me. He said something like "If you ever cross that line, you'll end up in Brackenridge," which was a hospital in Austin.

I think that I wrote so many songs with references to Clyde because he was so complicated. He could be comfortable in different worlds. He had this crazy sort of sophistication and intelligence to him, but at the same time he was a madman. He could bullshit his way into anything. He was charming and smart in that way. I couldn't brush him off like he never existed, because he was a big part of my life and I loved him, God bless him, and he loved me.

I was thinking about my duplex apartment in Silver Lake when I wrote the song "Right in Time." I had an image in my mind of this little kitchen with an old-fashioned stove and a woman who is thinking about her love interest. I started with the phrase "the way he moves is right in time" and went on from there. The man I was thinking about while writing that song was the guitarist Bo Ramsey, whose playing I loved and who I had an unconsummated crush on. I liked the way Bo moved, both onstage and offstage. So many of my songs start with one phrase or one image that I jot down in my notebooks and that I keep adding to. Sometimes the song will come together quickly; other times it takes years.

"Right in Time" grew into something else very quickly. It is about the yearnings and desires of a woman. I had a little mini-movie in my head. It follows a woman as she goes through her day: she turns off the lights as she's waiting for the water to boil on the stove, by herself, contemplating and daydreaming, and eventually she lies down on her bed and takes off her jewelry and begins sexually fantasizing and pleasuring herself. My mini-movie was in black and white, a bit noirish, lonely and haunted. She's found someone she has a connection with emotionally and physically, but she's not necessarily partnered with that person. She might not have ever met that person. Moving "right in time" could be sexual, real or imagined, or something else entirely, however anyone wants to interpret it.

Chattanooga, Tennessee, 1992.

The title song, "Car Wheels on a Gravel Road," originated from a dream I had one night. The line that came from the dream was "dogs barkin' in the yard." I started with that one line and I added a couple more lines. Then I fell asleep again, and when I woke up, I added a few more lines. This happened several nights in a row. So the song grew incrementally, not from an overarching vision. That's why I didn't realize that the child in the backseat crying was me.

I have very distinct and vivid memories of being a young girl in the backseat. Back then there was a flat space behind the front seat. There was no such thing as a car seat or seat belts or anything in those days. A small child could actually walk around behind the front seat while the car was moving. I remember one time my brother and sister were in the backseat with me and there were cotton fields as far as the eye could see and we wanted to stop and break off some cotton, so Dad stopped and he let us do it. The three of us kids were enthralled with the cotton fields that we came across on our excursions.

My father didn't make good money until he got his tenure job at the University of Arkansas, so our family car was this monster from the late 1940s or early 1950s. I used to call it "the fat car" because by the early 1960s cars started to be designed with sleek lines. The same thing happened to furniture and houses—sleek modern lines. Our car was big and round. I remember being kind of embarrassed by that car when I was in the third or fourth grade; by then I already had a sense of what was cool or not. I would hide in the backseat when I was dropped off at school.

"2 Kool 2 Be 4-Gotten" was inspired by a photograph in the Birney Imes photography book *Juke Joint*, which I found at the Davis-Kidd bookstore in Green Hills in Nashville. I would go to that store and spend hours browsing. It was a two-story store with a little café. That's also where I found a book called *Appalachian Portraits* by Shelby Lee Adams. When I first saw the Adams book, I thought the photographs must have been taken during the Depression, similar to work by Walker Evans and Dorothea Lange. But they were contemporary photographs. I was so impressed by Adams's work that I reached out to him and asked him to make photographs for the album.

I started writing "2 Kool" one morning in Knoxville. It was New Year's Day and I was hungover as fuck. My boyfriend at the time was Brian Waldschlager, a musician in a cool band called the Dirtclods. They played a hodgepodge of rock and hillbilly punk. I had driven over to Knoxville for a New Year's Eve show they were playing. There was a whole gang of us there. We were all drunk and we were dancing and somehow I ended up making out with a girl on the dance floor while Brian and the band were playing onstage. The next morning Brian told me that I'd embarrassed him the night before. "How?" I asked.

"By making out with that woman right in front of me and everybody," he said.

And I started writing "2 Kool" right that moment.

It's funny to think about that night now because I wonder

if the woman I kissed knew who I was. By then I was somewhat known; I'd been on *Austin City Limits,* for example, and the kinds of people that would have gone to that Dirtclods show might have known who I was. So I wonder if there's a woman out there in the world today who tells people, "I once made out with Lucinda Williams at a club during a show." Or maybe she had no idea who I was—she just wanted to kiss me.

The second part of "2 Kool" begins with "I had a lover, I, I thought he was mine." That's another reference to Clyde.

The line "That's your own death, you see" is meant to add a conversational quality to the song, as if I were talking to someone. There is a nice rhyme with "I told him, no way, baby, that's your own death, you see."

When I'm writing a song, I let my head go where it wants to go. Much of the process is stream of consciousness. I don't want to say I don't know how it happens, but it's almost impossible to put into words my process for writing songs. I don't always know where the songs come from and I almost never know where they are going. I put a tremendous amount of rigor into my work and then I let instinct make the decisions.

I don't just sit down with a blank sheet of paper and start at the beginning. I have all these references and notes that I carry around with me all the time, in a briefcase, and I might use them at any time. So something that might have gone into one song can end up in another song. Little snippets of things mix together in what becomes a song. I still carry this briefcase with me everywhere I go.

I started working on the song "Concrete and Barbed Wire" when the Berlin Wall was coming down. It was meant to be ironic. Why can't you tear down this wall? It's only made of concrete and barbed wire. I was imagining two lovers trapped on either side of the wall, trying to get back together. Of course, then the wall is metaphorical, not a literal wall. I started with the phrase "dogs are at the gate" and I was thinking about Clyde then, his love for Louisiana, and how he could break my heart but there were limits to his power. "Back in Algiers my darlin' broke my heart but he can't seem to break down this wall." I had been wanting to work the word "Algiers" into a song for some time and I finally found a way to use it in this one.

The inspiration for my song "Greenville" dates back to 1978, when I was recording my first Folkways album in Jackson, Mississippi, and living at Tom Royals's house. That October, I went to the blues festival in Greenville and met the forlorn Vietnam veteran with the guitar. I also ended up blending some images that came from knowing a singer-songwriter named Eric Taylor, who I met when I was playing sets at Anderson Fair in Houston. He was on the top end of an unstated local hierarchy of singer-songwriters in Houston. He would inevitably get drunk and start fights—you know, the same old story with these guys. Some people thought Eric was a genius; others thought he was an idiot.

He ended up marrying Nanci Griffith at some point, and when they split up, he tried to kill himself. He drank a bunch of whiskey and took some pills and turned the gas on in the stove and passed out next to it. He didn't die, because he forgot to close the windows and doors in the kitchen. I started writing a song about him and I later merged elements from that song into "Greenville." The songs had the same melody and the same tempo, so it made sense to combine them.

All during the time of writing and recording *Car Wheels,* I was deeply intrigued by snake handling in the southern mountains. The writer Dennis Covington published a book on that topic in 1995 called *Salvation on Sand Mountain.* And the novelist Lee Smith wrote a novel about the same subject, *Saving Grace,* that also came out in 1995.

I was proud of these songs and felt that they formed the strongest set of songs that I had written to that point in my career. Now we just had to record them.

16

I went ahead and signed with Rick Rubin's label, but as far as Gurf was concerned, he was to be co-producer of the new record with me, not Rick. I began to get a sense that Gurf's demands were holding me back. If he really wanted full control of his music, I felt he should go out on his own. At some point Rick pulled me aside and asked, "Have you ever thought of working with different musicians? Putting together a new band?" At first that idea scared the hell out of me. "Oh no," I told him. "This is my band. I'm loyal to them." I was protective of those guys. They had stuck with me while I got my career together in Los Angeles.

But the truth is that I had already started feeling a bit stifled. I wanted to avoid the conflict. Rick could see that this particular band had enjoyed a good run but that if I wanted to explore new creative areas, it might mean putting together a new one.

Despite these concerns, we started recording the new album later in 1995 with the same band and with Gurf in a production role. We started out working at Arlyn Studios in Austin, which was partly owned by Willie Nelson. Rick wasn't able to be in the studio with us, so we would ship tapes overnight to him in L.A. and then wait to hear his comments on the tracks.

This setup was doomed. The air was toxic. Gurf didn't want to hear what Rick had to say and I badly did. It was inevitable that Gurf and I would have a terrible falling-out—and we did. We agreed to take a break from recording and cool things down. I went back to Nashville. Conflicts are not uncommon among musicians during recording sessions—you're creating these recorded documents of your music that last forever—and often when musicians clash, all it takes is some distance to make things okay again. But I should have known that this situation would never be okay again.

After our break, Gurf and I went into Woodland Studios to overdub some vocals on a couple of tracks that weren't working. One of them was "Jackson," which is a very sensitive, almost gospel-like acoustic hymn that required a lot of care. It was also extra special to me, still one of my favorite songs to sing.

After a little while in the studio, I said, "Gurf, the track's not right. It's not working. We have to do something else." But he wouldn't listen. He insisted that we were making progress.

"Just do it again," he said, "just do it again."

"No, I'm not doing it again," I said. "It's not right." We kept butting heads. He went back to Austin and I stayed in Nashville and we took another break.

During this time I was having these stupid flirtations with various men. I remember this young writer who must have been fifteen or twenty years younger than me. One night we were standing in front of my house in Nashville, in the crisp fall air. I was trying to copy what I had seen my father do, having friends over to break bread. Thanksgiving heightened that desire to host for me, to be like my dad. Now I was with this younger writer who I had recently met. I wanted him to be brilliant and witty and I wanted to be in love. But he wasn't really brilliant and witty and I wasn't in love. Still, I was determined to make him into that vision I had. So we kissed and we kept kissing. I thought maybe I could turn him into a prince, a poet prince, someone my father would approve of, someone who would carry me with him on his journey through clouds of poetry, universities, and workshops. I was always on the lookout for the next genius poet. That's what I wanted, or what I thought I wanted. So I hung on. We kissed and we kissed some more. I would owe him apologies later. He would owe me nothing. We would meet again and share blushing moments and memories. Nothing more, nothing less.

A major, serendipitous career turning point came during this break when Steve Earle asked me to sing on his song "You're Still Standing There" on his album *I Feel Alright,* which would be released the following year. I went to Ray Kennedy's studio to record my vocals. Steve had worked with Ray on just about everything he'd ever done. Ray's studio was filled with vintage guitars and other vintage gear that he'd collected over the years. I'd say that he has a vintage way of doing things, even though he's also up to speed on all the modern technology. I loved the way my vocal sounded in Ray's production of Steve's song. Steve gave me a copy of the rough mixes for his album and I fell in love with the sound that Ray was getting. Bells went off in my head: this is it, this is how I want my record to sound.

At this point, we had rough mixes of all the songs that ended up on *Car Wheels.* Gurf thought we were ready for the final mixes. But when I played our rough mixes and then played Ray's rough mixes for Steve's album side by side, the sonic worlds were entirely different. I thought Steve's album sounded so much better than mine. I wanted to be in Ray and Steve's sonic world.

I played Steve's album for Gurf. I still hoped, perhaps senselessly, that he would continue to work with me in some capacity. "Gurf, listen to Steve's album," I said. "It sounds better than ours."

"I hate it," Gurf said. "I hate Steve's album. I hate his roughs. There's too much compression on it."

"I don't know what you call it," I said, "but whatever it is, I like it, and I like it better than what we have. So what are we going to do?"

I wanted to go with Steve and Ray. Gurf refused to recut the whole album. So I said, "Let's just recut 'Jackson.'" We had been struggling with that song for months. My bass player, John, and drummer, Donald, agreed. "Sure," they said, "let's go in and recut a couple of tracks with Steve and Ray. What the hell?"

That's how it started. We were just going to recut "Jackson" and everybody was in agreement except Gurf. What happened next was that the recuts sounded so great we got on a roll and ended up recutting the whole album.

Unfortunately, the tension between Gurf and me only increased. Something had to give. It was unsustainable. We decided to take another break. Gurf never came back and I never asked him to come back.

Making records can be so many things. It can be exciting. It can be tedious. It can be stressful. And it can be exhausting. It can test the limits and boundaries of everyone involved. I now understand that is normal.

Even with Gurf out of the circle, there was still pressure to finish the record, and some tension developed. I am very deliberate and I don't like to be rushed, and if I want to redo a vocal, I just want to be able to redo a vocal. No questions asked.

One day I came in to Ray's studio and I said to Steve and Ray, "I want to redo my vocal on 'Lake Charles.'" Steve said, "No, you don't need to do that. When are you going to trust someone, Lu?"

But I insisted and finally Steve blurted, "Lu, it's just a record for God's sakes, come on, get over it."

"It's not *just* a record," I said. He thought I was underestimating myself, that he knew better, and to be fair, he also thought I was brilliant and he said so, but he also said I was driving him crazy. One night I ended up bursting into tears and lying in the fetal position in my vocal booth. I had trouble feeling overwhelmed with pressure occasionally and one of my fight-flight responses would be to just check out in whatever way I could.

A few days later Steve arrived at the studio and he said, "I'm done. That's it. I'm fucking buying a ticket to New Orleans and I'm getting the fuck out of here. I've had it." He didn't actually leave, but he made his point. He stayed and eventually we got everything done and then left to go on the road.

But I still felt there were a few more things on the record that needed to be added.

My bass player, John, was friends with Roy Bittan, longtime keyboard player in the E Street Band, and he suggested we reach out to Roy for the final touches. Roy was doing his own engineering and production work in Los Angeles whenever he wasn't on the road with Springsteen and he told John he'd be happy to work with us. We flew out to L.A. and we worked with Roy at Rumbo Studios in Canoga Park.

We finally finished the album, despite all the drama with Gurf and the tension between me and Steve, all the different studios and different cities, and all the recording costs piling up. I thought we were finally at the finish line. Then, unbelievably, a big new obstacle arose. The label that Rick Rubin owned, American, was in the process of switching distribution companies and Rick decided to hold *Car Wheels* until the new distribution arrangement was completed.

Rick held up the album for two years.

By this point, five years had passed since *Sweet Old World* and there was still no new record from me. Rumors were flying about how difficult I was to work with. There was a long, horrendous feature story on me in *The New York Times Magazine* that unfairly threw gasoline on those rumors. The writer made me out to be a control-obsessed lunatic. The title of his article was "Lucinda Williams Is in Pain." To my knowledge the writer had never written about the process of making records before and he had no idea how messy it almost always is. Yes, this process had been particularly fraught, and I'm well aware that there are times when I can bring an extra layer of unpredictable emotion to a situation that is already tough to begin with. I had a vision I was committed to executing properly. Sometimes it's not easy to communicate that kind of vision, and if musicians you've known for years are struggling to understand you, then there is no way an outsider can. When Emmylou Harris heard this story later, she gave me some important advice: never let a writer into your recording studio. I learned that lesson the hard way.

During this whole time I played as many shows as I could, to generate some income and to enjoy myself. A lot of people, including my friends in the music business and on my team, were reaching out to Rick asking him about my record. People were very upset with him; they felt he was doing a lot of damage to my career by holding the album. But that didn't strike a chord with Rick. Finally, my manager, Frank Callari, who had known Rick from their early New York days, decided to take a different approach. He knew of Rick's spiritual side and Frank shared that interest. Frank called Rick one night at home, and he said, "Dude, you gotta do this, man. It's a spiritual thing. Look into your third eye, Rick, look into your third eye, and tell me you don't see that Lu's record has to be put out there."

"I see," said Rick, and he agreed to release the record.

But my record still hadn't found its home. There was another unforeseen kink in the process.

My attorney for virtually my whole career and still today, Rosemary Carroll, had given a copy of the record to her husband, Danny Goldberg, who was the head of Mercury Records, and Danny loved it. He loved it so much he convinced the powers that be at Mercury to write a check for $450,000 to buy my contract from Rick at American. I didn't know the details of this deal until many years later. All I knew was there was a good label excited to release the record sooner than Rick had in mind.

When the record went into production at Mercury, we had to make decisions on the packaging and cover art, which was another drama. The Mercury PR people hesitated about my desire to use Shelby Lee Adams's photos but ultimately said okay. Adams was from eastern Kentucky but he lived in Boston and taught at one of the colleges there. He came down to Nashville and brought one assistant with him to help carry equipment. Mercury sent several PR people down from New York for the shoot.

I did my own hair and makeup and we found an old tire lot in Nashville and other locations and spent a day getting photos of me. The New York PR people had never seen a photographer work like Adams. He's not a photo-shoot photographer like Danny Clinch (who I love) going *click, click, click, click* all day long. Adams uses large slow-exposure cameras and everything happens very slowly, one photograph at a time. I could tell the PR people were getting very impatient. The next day they set up their own shoot with stylists and makeup artists and the whole huge New York photo-shoot apparatus.

I didn't want the PR photos in the album; I wanted Shelby Adams's and Birney Imes's photos. I was having a hard time making the final decisions about which of their photos to use, and I knew I was going to have to make a big push with the PR people to get what I wanted. I remember sitting in my kitchen in Nashville and my attorney, Rosemary, called me and said, "Lucinda, look, I don't care if this record comes out in a brown paper bag. You need to decide today which art you want on the record." End of story. I chose the Imes picture for the cover and the Adams picture for the back cover. Mercury thankfully agreed to go with my choices.

Car Wheels was finally released in 1998, six years after *Sweet Old World*. It won a Grammy for Best Contemporary Folk Album and it is still my best-selling record today.

But the label of obsessive perfectionist has haunted me ever since.

The veteran music writer Holly George-Warren later wrote an essay in my defense and said, "The issue goes beyond an artist being held to task for taking too long to finish a record. A lot of things I've heard said about Lucinda are sexist—that she's difficult, for example. You don't hear things like that about Bruce Springsteen or John Fogerty. Both of them have taken a long time to make records." She went on: "It seems that happens a lot, especially if a woman hears things a certain way—her way—rather than the way a male producer tells her they should sound."

A painful part of the aftermath of the *Car Wheels* drama that lasts until today is my relationship with Gurf. It happened twenty-five years ago and he still won't talk to me today. I don't really know why and he won't tell anyone, even mutual friends. He still maintains that his mixes of *Car Wheels* are better than what came out and he says so publicly.

I have held out an olive branch to Gurf several times. A few years ago Tom and I went to a show Gurf was playing at a small club in L.A. This was not too long after our original band's bass player, John Ciambotti, had passed away. Our drummer, Donald Lindley, had passed away a decade earlier, so Gurf and I were the only remaining members of the band. Both deaths were sudden. I thought maybe it was finally the right time to patch things up with Gurf. Plus, Tom had never met him. I was hoping that we might be able to clear the air. I made the effort to go check out his show and I thought that might mean something to him. But instead, he dusted us off. Then he emailed me the next day and said, "Please stay out of my life." Tom was furious, and if you mention Gurf to Tom today, he still gets riled up. It's something that has broken my heart for a long time, but now I can accept that we can never mend fences even if I still ask myself, "How can someone be that bitter after all these years?"

17

When *Car Wheels* was being prepared for release, Danny Goldberg had the idea of having the filmmaker Paul Schrader make a video or a short film based on "Right in Time." I normally declined to make videos for any of my songs, but Schrader had made some reputable movies and written scripts in association with Martin Scorsese for movies like *Raging Bull* and *Taxi Driver* and all that. He also made a movie that he directed himself, *Mishima,* that had some good music in it, music composed by Philip Glass and performed by the classical string group the Kronos Quartet. I'm no film authority but I agreed that this sounded like an idea worth talking about. Schrader flew down to Nashville to meet with me and discuss it.

I had a photo shoot earlier in the day and I went straight to meet Schrader from the shoot. We met at the Sunset Grill. My boyfriend at the time, Richard Price (the bass player, not the novelist and TV writer), met us there, too. It was obvious that Schrader had been drinking heavily. He probably drank on the plane on the flight down from New York. I sat down at the table and Richard excused himself to go use the bathroom before sitting down. Schrader turned to me and leaned over, and the first thing he said to me was, "If I weren't so fucked up right now, I'd probably try to get inside your pants."

The phrase "sex, drugs, and rock and roll" suggests that the only people who get out of hand and behave in questionable ways are rock-and-roll musicians. But in my experience musicians are a clean-living lot compared with the aforementioned people in the literary world and the people I later met in Hollywood. I've spent a lot of time with male musicians over many years and most of them keep things professional.

When Richard returned to our table from the bathroom, I should have gotten up and walked out. But we stayed and ate dinner. Then we went to a bar in the Printer's Alley area of Nashville called Skull's. For a long time it was a legendary bar in town. When we arrived at Skull's, I went to the bathroom and Schrader turned to Richard and said, "When you are back at home later tonight and you and Lucinda are in bed, I want you to tell her you think my ideas for this video are good. Try to convince her with some sweet pillow talk."

When Richard told me that later, I laughed. This guy thinks I'm going to be a pushover like that? In the music business, people had learned not to try to fuck with me because it's not going to work, ever.

Schrader wanted to set the video in a 1940s antiques store being run by a husband and wife, and I would be the wife. Then the husband would be called off to war in Europe and the wife would be left alone. The night before he left, the couple would be filmed dancing around the antiques shop.

I told Schrader that when I wrote "Right in Time," I imagined a noirish black-and-white video of a woman alone in her apartment with lots of oblique shots of her ending up in the bedroom, taking off her bracelets and earrings and lying back on the bed and doing her thing, although you wouldn't be able to really see it on camera, just oblique glimpses.

"Oh, that's too dark," said Schrader, "we can't do that."

"What about the popular Nirvana video," I asked, "with dark black-and-white imagery like that?"

"Yeah, but they're Nirvana," he said. "They can do that. You can't."

He also said that before he flew down to Nashville, Danny had told him, "I know Lucinda is going to want to do something dark and arty. Don't let her."

There was no way I was going to work with Schrader. He was just another guy trying to impose his vision on a female artist. *Car Wheels* did fine without a video.

After *Car Wheels* finally came out, my career shifted into a different gear. I signed a contract for a new six-album deal with Lost Highway, which was a part of Mercury run by Luke Lewis, who was always wonderful to work with, really smart and genuine. Basically I had to make an album a year for six years. The whole structure of my life changed. I had more money, we had two tour buses, and I had more obligations. I had this steady thing for the first time in my life. I was in my late forties and I was ready for it. Before this my work had been erratic and my life chaotic. Now things were happening in a consistent way and I could look a bit further down the road. I don't remember feeling any pressure to produce six new albums. It felt exciting.

Nashville was turning into a party scene toward the end of the 1990s. That's when Ryan Adams moved to town. It was a big deal that he moved to Nashville because young musicians like him usually moved to L.A. or New York. He was around twenty-five years old and had been the leader of the important country rock band Whiskeytown. This was before he released any of his solo stuff. At the time Frank Callari was managing both Ryan and me.

A year or so after *Car Wheels* had come out, Frank took me to hear Ryan at a popular joint in Nashville called 12th and Porter, which had a restaurant on one side and a small performance venue on the other. Ryan was by himself, just him and his guitar and his harmonica, wearing jeans and a T-shirt and a denim jacket, like he dresses pretty much all the time. He started playing and I stood there completely in awe. I remember standing next to Frank and watching this kid—he was a kid, really—singing these amazing songs with a certain kind of presence and projection. He played some songs that eventually turned up on his first solo record, *Heartbreaker,* which I still think is a great record. I turned to Frank and said, "Oh my God, he's a genius." After that I was smitten and impressed with everything about him. Apparently, he was impressed with me, too. He knew my records.

Ryan loved Frank and I loved Frank, too, so it was quite natural for all of us to hang out together. One night we were at some bar, a bunch of us, including Frank and Ryan, and two girls who worked for Frank. Back then, when I wanted to drink, I ordered beer with shots of tequila. I preferred wine but you couldn't get wine worth drinking in a bar in Nashville then. Ryan turned me on to vodka tonics and that was the beginning of the end.

What happened between Ryan and me is almost irrelevant because it wasn't a real love affair. It was just a flirtation. Ryan loved to flirt and so did I. Flirting is very underrated. Ryan was twenty-one years younger than I was, but that didn't matter.

We connected on all sorts of levels musically and intellectually; there was instant appreciation and understanding.

But with our age difference, the possibility of a serious relationship wasn't there at all, so nobody was thinking about that. It was impossible. But that impossibility is also something that allows things to happen.

After a few vodka tonics one night, when we were laughing and having a good time, Ryan leaned over to me and said, "We need to go somewhere and make out." So we went to the courtyard outside the bar and we started rolling around and kissing. At some point I bit his lip. That's just how I am in heated situations like that and plenty of guys enjoy it. Then I bit his lip again. He pulled away and said, "Don't bite." I said, "Sorry," and he just got up and walked away and left. I didn't hear from him again for many months.

18

I remember listening to other artists when I was young and thinking, "I don't want everything to sound the same. I want to be eclectic and use different styles." What I wanted to be was someone like Bob Dylan or Neil Young, who could pretty much do whatever they wanted. Not many women are given that opportunity. Everybody wants to keep them contained in some sort of predetermined box. Bob Dylan and Neil Young can do all sorts of albums in all sorts of styles but it's still them. That's what I wanted to be, even from a young age. My husband, Tom, recently told me that he read something where someone said, "All of Lucinda's records are different but at the center they always retain Lucinda." I take it as the ultimate compliment.

I wanted to move in a different direction with my next album. I'd won a Grammy with *Car Wheels,* so I felt like a lot of people would expect a similar follow-up, but I wanted to do something else. Fans get really attached to the narrative songs on *Car Wheels*—"Drunken Angel" and "Lake Charles" and "Greenville"—I think because they feel like they know somebody like those characters. But I wanted to get away from narrative songs and put even more emphasis on how the whole thing sounded. I wanted to make an album where the music dominates the song rather than the lyrics dominating the song—more about a vibe and a groove than a story to be told. But I was in a bind: I knew that if I made a record like *Car Wheels,* some people would say, this is like *Car Wheels* but not as good. If I made something different, then some people would say, it doesn't sound like *Car Wheels* so it's not as good.

I'm not sure what in my makeup caused me to take this risk and change my style from something that had been, finally, very successful to something new, but it was the most important transition of my career. When I started working on the song "Are You Down," which has very few lyrics compared with my earlier songs, I remember thinking, "Wow, I like this, but can I really make records with songs like this?" It was a breakthrough when I realized that I could.

If I'm honest, one thing that might have pushed me in this direction was that after *Car Wheels* came out, everybody started lumping me in with Americana or alt-country, and I can't stand either of those terms, as I said before. They are so limiting. I realize that people were trying to be complimentary, but it still bothered me, so on some level I said to myself, "I'm going to do something different." That's just my nature.

When I had the songs for *Essence* written, I sent them to my father, as I always did, because sometimes he'd have little suggestions for changing a word here and there, and who's kidding who, I was also after his approval, which is something I've had to work through in therapy. I was nervous about sending him these new songs because they were so different, with fewer words overall. After he read the lyrics, he called me and said, "Honey, this is the closest you've come to pure poetry yet."

"Really?" I said.

"Yeah, you've graduated."

I remember he used that term, "graduated," and it caused me to look back at my career and find other points where I had graduated and gone on to bigger and better and more independent things. I didn't feel a need to keep sending my songs to my dad after that.

While I was working on the songs for *Essence,* Dylan's album *Time Out of Mind,* produced by Daniel Lanois, came out and I loved it. It was beautiful lyrically and musically and sonically. That's the kind of sound and feel I was looking for on my next record. I was also listening to Sade's album *Lovers Rock,* which came out in 2000. It had a feel to it that was maintained over a wide variety of music on the album, from reggae and dub to rock to folk and soul and R&B.

I was a nomad in music and a nomad in life: around this time I moved back to Los Angeles. A writer and musician friend of mine, Nicholas Hill, had a radio show at a really cool station in East Orange, New Jersey, and you could pick it up in New York City. I would listen whenever I was in the area. He played a lot of independent artists that played blues and folk and rock and was always discovering new talent. He came to L.A. right after I moved back and he gave me a CD by Mia Doi Todd. I remember when we were driving in his rental car and he put the CD into the car's player. Immediately I was struck. She is unique. Her music was in the vein of Suzanne Vega. Very simple and stark. She was another inspiration.

A while later, I was in a record store and I noticed that Todd's latest record had been released on a different label, a smaller label, than the previous one. It made me think, "Okay, I know what's going on here. She's probably getting the runaround from the labels, getting jerked around." I don't know if that's exactly what happened to her but I could see it being the case—she is so unique nobody would know what to do with her—and it inspired one of my songs, "Rarity," that was released on my album *Little Honey* in 2008.

> You are a rarity
> Your eyes say wisdom
> Your skin says frailty
> Your mouth says listen

Lucinda Williams

Your voice a cello
Your words speak volumes
In and out around flow
Like Leonard Cohen's

Since you were invented
Since you came along
No one's even attempted
To come close to the beauty of your song

No hits on the radio
No one knows who you are
No big deal with a video
So you're never gonna be a star

You won't be attending
Meetings with presidents
Of companies pretending
To protect their investments

While they suck the gristle
Off the bones of your art
Unfaithful and fickle
Seductive and smart

They'll say you're a rarity
And sleep in your bed
And strangle your purity
And leave you for dead

They'll call you little honey
And write you a check
Seduce you with money
And fuck your respect

For offering a small glimpse
Through your secret door
Of your intellect and brilliance
You deserve so much more

'Cause you, you're a rarity
Your eyes say wisdom
Your skin says frailty
Your mouth says listen

Some people have told me that I was brave to try something new, but I was actually scared shitless at the time. I didn't know if it was going to work and I had this big new contract with Lost Highway. The stakes were higher. It would be extremely embarrassing if my first album for them was a dud. They signed me based on the success of *Car Wheels* and the Rough Trade record. This new record would be nothing like either of those.

I already had "Blue" and "Bus to Baton Rouge," which were old, old, old songs, and I thought I'd put those on the record to satisfy the people who wanted the narrative stuff, but I could record them in a new way and the rest of the record would be all about the groove.

The recording of *Essence* happened relatively fast. I made a demo of the songs with the guitarist Bo Ramsey, just the two of us. It was a thrill in more ways than musically because I'd always sort of had a crush on him, so it was fun for me to be around him. I sent the demo to Lost Highway and Luke Lewis flipped out. He said, "This is so good we could release the record just like this." So we agreed that Bo would produce the album with me. I was elated.

I didn't want to record with my touring band at that time. We had just spent two years on the road and those guys were incredible, but I felt like we'd perfected the sound that I was now trying to move on from.

Bo and my manager, Frank Callari, suggested a bunch of different musicians and we ended up with a remarkable band for the sessions. We got Dylan's bassist, Tony Garnier, and his guitarist, Charlie Sexton, and we got the legendary drummer Jim Keltner, and Bo and Ryan Adams played guitar, too. Jim Lauderdale sang harmony vocals on the record, as he had done on *Car Wheels*.

Before we started recording, Bo and Frank and I went to visit the engineer Jim Dickinson, who had produced the Replacements' breakthrough record, *Pleased to Meet Me*. He was living with his wife in a trailer in Coldwater, Mississippi, which is near Memphis. They had bought a bunch of property and put a trailer on it with the intention of building a nice house. But it had been a few years and they hadn't broken ground yet. There was also a recording studio on the property. We thought we might want to record there, but Jim hadn't gotten it in working order. I've never had a baby, so I can't really speak to that experience, but I imagine that when a woman has a baby, she has in mind a perfect location for the birthing. That's sort of like how I feel about making records in certain places, always thinking about the perfect place to make a record. Jim's place wasn't it. He also wasn't prepared for our meeting. He hadn't listened to my records and didn't seem to really know who I was. So we thanked him for his time and left.

Bo mentioned a man named Tom Tucker who had a studio called Master Mix in Minneapolis. Bo had worked on a lot of records with Greg Brown in that studio. Tom had also done significant engineering for Prince in Prince's studio. I loved and respected Bo and I immediately agreed. So we found some time when the whole band could meet there and I sent the duo demo that Bo and I had made in Nashville to all the musicians so they could learn the songs.

Everything seemed easier and better than ever. I drove my Chevy Silverado pickup truck all the way to Minneapolis. I've always loved driving across the country by myself. It was October, a beautiful time of year, and I watched the leaves gradually change colors as I made it farther north. I stayed in a motel off the highway about halfway there and made the drive in two days.

We cut the basic tracks of *Essence* in about ten days. Once we were all in Minneapolis, we were on a tight deadline because

Jim Keltner had to go back out on the road with Neil Young and Charlie Sexton and Tony Garnier had to go back out with Dylan. As a result there was some tinkering left to be done after those guys left, a few mistakes that needed to be fixed without the musicians still with us.

Bo and I weren't sure what to do. Bo suggested that we bring some local Minneapolis musicians he knew into the studio to do some overdubs, but I didn't want to do that. So we had a little bit of a problem about how to move forward.

Tom Tucker had found a young guy who was a whiz kid at Pro Tools, which was early computer software used by many audio and video editors. This was my first experience with Pro Tools and this kid was brilliant at it. Also, I was able to get Charlie Sexton on the phone and he had a couple of days off from Dylan's tour, so he flew back to Minneapolis. The combination of those three guys saved the day. It was basically like surgery with Charlie, Tom, and the whiz kid taking different pieces from different takes and putting the puzzle together. It was astounding what they did. I'd never seen anything like it. The resulting sound on the record was exactly what I had envisioned.

I love that album. Today, a lot of people come up to me and tell me that *Essence* is their favorite one of my records. I try not to pick favorites, but I understand when someone says that.

———————

The mixing and mastering of *Essence* took place over the Thanksgiving and Christmas seasons. I stayed in Minneapolis by myself. I moved out of a vintage hotel and into an Extended Stay hotel, where I had a suite with a kitchen. It was the first time in my life that I'd spent Christmas by myself. I had heard that one shouldn't spend Christmas alone, but I thought it would be no big deal for me; it's just another day.

When I was around twenty-one, my father and stepmother went to Rome for Christmas, so I was in New Orleans with my mother and my brother. One day Mom was into her drugs and drinking and I had to get out of the apartment. I was of legal age and I wandered into a bar on Christmas Eve. It was the first time I'd ever been in a bar by myself. In an odd way I felt liberated because I didn't have to deal with my family. My father and stepmother were in another country and my mother had checked out for the day and night. I remember feeling, "Wow, this is kind of cool in an odd sort of way." It was the first time I remember realizing that I enjoyed being alone. And it has been true for most of my life.

Tom Tucker's family had looked after me during those winter months in Minneapolis, when we were working on the mixes in the studio. They gave me a little Christmas tree and some decorations for my hotel room. Everything was fine until Christmas Day. I felt a different kind of melancholy than I normally feel. The day went by so slowly. It was like the clock was going backward. I made it through, but I was left thinking that I didn't want to spend the holidays alone again.

As Tom and I were working to finalize *Essence,* Bo Ramsey was in and out of Minneapolis working with us as needed. Living in nearby Iowa, he could go back and forth easily. I'd had a crush on Bo for a long time and I decided on one of his visits that I was going to try to make something happen between us. I went out and bought candles and incense for my hotel room, and I ordered some good food and wine to be delivered and I invited him to my room to "work on the album." I put a lot of thought into what I was going to wear and what I was going to say in trying to seduce him.

Bo arrived at my room and candles and incense were lit. I had Sade playing on the boom box. My seduction efforts went completely over his head, or beside his head, or something. He showed absolutely no inclination to return my amorous efforts and kept the evening purely focused on the record and our careers.

A few years later Bo and I crossed paths and I reminded him that I had tried to have sex with him. He said, "What? Why didn't you tell me that's what you were doing? I would have been happy to oblige."

I missed my chance. By this time Bo was married to Greg Brown's daughter Pieta. But at least we'd made a damn good record.

19

I had not seen Ryan Adams since that night he walked away in Nashville a few years earlier, but when I was in Minneapolis recording *Essence,* he showed up. Frank Callari was still managing both of us and Ryan came to town to play some gigs. We were all staying in the same hotel. It was an old mill downtown that had been converted into a cool vintage hotel. With all the musicians in town, the hotel became party central.

When I first saw Ryan, he was in the lobby looking disheveled and unruly, with his jeans and T-shirt and denim jacket, hair a dirty mop. He was sitting there reading section A of *The New York Times,* holding the paper spread out in front of him, really focused on it. So, yet again, here's this mix of qualities I find so appealing, the roughneck intellectual, the poet on a motorcycle. Here's this guy who is a borderline disaster and he's seriously reading section A of *The New York Times,* not the arts section or the sports section or even the business section. Ryan saw me, put the paper down, and immediately started up the same flirty thing with me again.

I had decided I was going to make him say "I'm sorry" for deserting me that night at the bar in Nashville and never calling me again or responding to any of my casual overtures that I sent through Frank. Ryan was such a golden child, like he could do no wrong, and I was going to make him say "I'm sorry." He resisted. He didn't want to say it. It was like pulling teeth trying to get him to admit that he fucked up. But he finally did. The next day he went to a bookstore in Minneapolis and brought me back a book of Sylvia Plath's letters, which had just come out, and he jotted a note to me inside it.

After three days in Minneapolis we went our separate ways and were barely in touch after that. That's all that happened. We never had sex. But our encounters did inspire a song. I wrote "Those Three Days," which came out on *World Without Tears* in 2003. It isn't a literal description of what happened. In fact, I still can't make sense of what happened between us. People have told me that they relate to it, maybe because it's so hard to make sense of attraction.

You say there's always gonna be this thing
Between us days are filled with dreams

Scorpions crawl across my screen

Make their home beneath my skin

Underneath my dress stick their tongues

Bite through the flesh down to the bone

And I have been so fucking alone

Since those three days.

Did you only want me for those three days?

Did you only need me for those three days?

Did you love me forever

Just for those three days?

You built a nest inside my soul

You rest your head on leaves of gold

You managed to crawl inside my brain

You found a hole and in you came

You sleep like a baby breathing

Comfortably between truth and pain

But the truth is nothing's been the same

Since those three days.

The next time I saw Ryan was at SXSW in Austin a few years later. We were both still being managed by Frank and we were playing at the same venue on the same day. Ryan ended up on my tour bus with me parked outside the venue. Some other people were there and we were talking and drinking. I was drinking Grand Marnier. There was gin and vodka around. Ryan and I started flirting and talking and flirting and talking and I completely forgot that the next morning I was meeting the celebrated photographer Annie Leibovitz for a photo shoot. I'm getting shit-faced with Ryan Adams and I'm going to look like hell the next morning for this important shoot. At some point I got up to go to the bathroom and when I came back out Ryan was gone. Classic Ryan.

Somehow I made it to the Hotel San José, where we—my band and traveling crew—were staying. I passed out on the couch in my suite wearing all my clothes. I woke up with a horrible hangover and I'm thinking, "Fuck, I've got to meet Annie Leibovitz for this photo shoot and I'm fucking hungover and look awful." So I took a shower. I washed my hair, which I never do before photo shoots. I learned that lesson years ago: Don't ever wash your hair before you do a photo shoot. Leave it dirty.

Annie showed up at my suite at the San José at the planned time. She took one look at me and the first thing she said was, "Oh . . ." And then there was a long pause that was a little bit awkward. I had just come out of the shower and my clothes were on but I hadn't put on any makeup or anything. She said, "I'd love to photograph you right now the way you are."

"No, no," I said. "I have a makeup artist. I have a stylist. I have all that." She didn't care.

"Look, I'm fucked up as shit," I told Annie. "I'm hungover as shit and I feel like crap."

"That's okay," she said, "just do whatever you want. Look down, look away, put your sunglasses on, pull your jacket up over your head, I don't care."

I had never worked with a photographer who didn't make me stand there and smile when I didn't feel like smiling. She didn't care if I was smiling or not. She knew how I was feeling and she didn't force me into some other pose or position. It didn't make sense to me at the time. But then, when I saw the photographs later, I thought, "Oh my God, this is why she is so good."

With most of the photographers I work with, you can tell if a certain shot is going to be cool or not while it is being shot. With Annie, you can't tell anything. She told me that whenever she shoots someone, the subject always says, "This is the worst shoot I've ever had. Nothing cool is going to come out of this." Then, when they see the photos, they can't believe it.

A while after that shoot, Annie came to Nashville and stopped by my house. She just wanted to hang out and I welcomed it. I was renting one of those three-level condo things and my office was on the third floor. That's where I kept all my books and stuff. She came up there and she noticed that I had a copy of her iconic *Rolling Stone* book that had come out years ago. She says, "Oh, yeah, I pretty much fucked everybody in that book," or something like that. I have no idea whether she was being serious. I know she's a lesbian, or I guess she's bi. I don't know. It doesn't matter. People fuck people. Whatever. Who cares?

Ryan and I didn't stay in touch after that night before the photo shoot. At the time he was having problems. He wasn't reliable and dependable, in the way a friend would be. My relationship with him was very brief, but it was important to me. I loved him. I still do. After the allegations arose around 2019 about sexual misconduct in his past, I thought the right thing to do was reach out to him. I called him and he said, "I hope you don't think I'm a monster."

"I don't think you are a monster, Ryan," I said. "I think you just made some bad choices."

20

After *Essence* came out, we started seeing some crazy stuff from the stage. I guess I'd developed a sort of fringe cult following among some of my fans. At the first Jazz Fest in New Orleans after Katrina, we were playing the song "Essence" at the House of Blues and there was a woman off to the side of the stage openly masturbating. Security grabbed her and pulled her out and she never stopped rubbing herself as she was being hauled out. Then there was this couple who came to many of my shows and the man had my name tattooed on his arm. They sent my manager a negligee with these little panties to give to me. It was the weirdest thing. Otherwise they looked like a normal middle-aged couple. Another guy had the entire lyrics of my song

"Blessed" tattooed on his back and he walked up to the front of the stage and took his shirt off to show me. One time we were playing a show in Macon, Georgia, and somebody figured out where we were staying and delivered a paper bag of Vidalia onions to my room. There was another guy who wanted my signature so he could get it tattooed on him. I could go on and on. The way I see it, this kind of fan attention is the ultimate honor.

After *Essence,* some rumors started that I was doing hard drugs like heroin. I'm not sure how they began. I think part of it had to do with the subject matter of some of my songs. And then on *World Without Tears* there are a couple of references to heroin. But I've never been into hard drugs.

Once around that time I had a show in Denver. I think it was the first time I'd ever played a show at altitude and I wasn't aware of its effects. We were staying at a Kimpton Hotel and there was an Aveda salon in the lobby with all these services. I had this incredible massage, but you don't want to do that before a show; you want to do that after a show. After the massage, I ordered room service and I had a couple of glasses of wine, which I typically do before shows. But this time the combination of the relaxation from the massage, the altitude, and the wine made me woozy onstage. A few fans who attended the show wrote something about it on the internet, wondering if I was strung out. Then, not long after that, I was doing an interview with a journalist and he asked me, "When did you get out of rehab?"

"What?" I said.

"You were in drug rehab, weren't you?"

"You've got the wrong person," I said.

The closest I came to using hard drugs was when I was living in Austin in 1974 or 1975. Drugs were just flowing. You didn't even have to buy pot or mushrooms; they were just always around, always available wherever you went. I was living in a house with roommates and decided I would try amphetamines and I kind of liked them. A little upper for a woman who had been a depressive child. They were these little pills that people called white crosses. I'd have one of them every once in a while when I was smoking pot and I liked the feeling of that mix. But I didn't do it for very long. For one thing, you had to have money to buy hard drugs and I didn't have any money.

Once, when I had some extra money, I thought I would try crystal meth. There was this guy around Austin who was selling pure crystal meth. He reminded me of Ginger Baker, with long hair and huge eyes that were always wide open. He was a speed freak but everybody liked him because he was always smiling and having fun. I called him and he showed up at our house and brought out this huge fucking bag of crystal meth and it scared the hell out of me. I remember thinking that it wasn't controllable doses and I didn't know how much you were supposed to take. I told him I'd changed my mind. I've always felt that I've had a little angel on one shoulder and a little devil on the other. This time the little angel won. I stepped away once and for all from hard drugs. Over all these years I've settled mostly for wine, and sometimes mixed drinks.

Granted, there have been a few times when I've had a bit too much, not unlike my father and his writer friends when they had those literary parties at our house in Fayetteville. Still today, one of my joys is gathering with a few friends and having a few drinks and breaking bread together.

21

E*ssence* was released in June 2001 and my next album, *World Without Tears,* was released less than two years later, in April 2003. During those years we toured nonstop. I wrote *World Without Tears* on the road. Those songs poured out of me. My life was hectic and stressful then, but in a good way. My career was skyrocketing and new opportunities were happening.

I moved out of Nashville and back to Los Angeles. It was another of my restless, nomadic moves. When I wasn't touring, I was living at the Safari Inn in Burbank, a great motel built in the 1950s. It had been carefully renovated over the years. It was my favorite place to stay when I was back in L.A. Usually I could get the same room, an efficiency with a kitchen and a separate bedroom and living room. They'd give me a special rate for an extended stay. There was a good restaurant with room service. That's pretty much all I needed. I'm not sure why, but I feel free spirited when I stay in motels or hotels. I've always imagined residing in a hotel. I remember reading about Lauren Bacall's apartment in New York City, which was described as comfortable and elegant.

I turned fifty a few months before *World Without Tears* was released. Most of the songs on that album were inspired by men I'd had brief but potent relationships with.

One of them was a bartender named Billy Mercer, who I met at 12th and Porter toward the end of my time living in Nashville, the same venue where I first saw Ryan Adams play. He'd played bass in Ryan's band at some point, but he wasn't a full-time musician.

The night Joey Ramone died, I was drinking at 12th and Porter and Billy was bartending. After a while his shift was over and a few of us went to another joint called the Slow Bar. Everybody was getting hammered and feeling emotional about Joey Ramone dying. We were singing Ramones songs and dancing around. Billy and I ended up in the bathroom of the Slow Bar making out like savage beasts. When we left, I went with him to his place.

Billy and I were 100 percent incompatible—he was nineteen years younger and in a very different place in his life— but we had an unbeatable chemistry. When I met him, I didn't know how young he was and frankly I didn't care. He was soulful and, most of the time, sweet. He had big blue eyes and dark eyelashes. My time with Billy inspired the songs "Fruits of My Labor," "Righteously," "Overtime," "Sweet Side," and "People Talkin'." But the relationship was going nowhere in a personal or intimate way. It just petered out.

My song "Ventura" was written in the middle of the Billy and Ryan time period, but it's not really about them so much. I wrote that song thinking about Neil Young's record *Everybody Knows This Is Nowhere,* which is one of my all-time favorite records. So much of Neil's stuff feels like the ocean to me, the sound of waves, and it's haunting. There's also a sort of aloneness to his sound and his music on that record. I wanted to get at something like that.

Twenty years after *World Without Tears* came out, I was collaborating with the great jazz saxophonist Charles Lloyd and he told me that "Ventura" was one of his favorite songs of mine. He knew all my stuff, which was flattering, but the comment about "Ventura" meant a lot because Charles is from Memphis but for many years he's lived in Santa Barbara, so he's got a southern and Southern California mix similar to what I have.

I wrote "Real Live Bleeding Fingers and Broken Guitar Strings" after spending time with Paul Westerberg, lead singer of the Replacements. It was another short-lived liaison. He had apparently been admiring me from a distance for years. Sometimes when I was playing shows at joints like Al's Bar or Raji's or the Troubadour in my early days in L.A., the Replacements would be on the same weekend bill as me.

I remember going to see them play at the Palace in L.A. and they were loud and drunk and awesome. Then, a few years later, somebody gave me Paul's solo album *14 Songs* and I absolutely fell in love with that record and his other solo recordings.

Somehow or another Paul and I managed to connect and I saw him a few times when he came to L.A. We talked on the phone and I went to his shows. He got shit-faced drunk at one of his shows and he wanted me to sit in with him on one of his songs. He was always so fucked up. I heard he went into recovery later. Spending time with him, I got a little peek behind the scenes of the drunk rock star guy. I remember sitting in his hotel room one time and there was a knock on the door and there were two giggly girls outside expecting to come in. Paul must have given them his room number backstage after the show. I thought, "Wow, this is going to be one of those kinds of things. Here I am in my late forties and well established and this kind of thing is going on right in front of me."

My relationship with Paul didn't last very long, because he was so inconsistent, so much of a hound dog. He was a mess. But he had those same qualities that always attract me—intelligence and talent. At one point he was telling me about what was going on with his wife and their son and I told him, "Look, you need to go see a therapist to sort all this stuff out." He didn't like that. He was seriously mad. I said, "See ya later." It was over.

"Atonement" was inspired by the movie based on Flannery O'Connor's novel *Wise Blood*. There's a preacher in the song, not unlike my maternal grandfather, with the hellfire and brimstone, trying to cram religion down your throat, especially with that line "Lock you in a room with a holy roller and a one-man band." In *Wise Blood* the main character's father is a preacher and the character has frequent flashbacks.

"World Without Tears" is simply a statement about life and pain. That's a song I always perform when there's been a tragedy in the country, which now seems to happen every week.

Stylistically, I knew I wanted *World Without Tears* to rock harder than anything I'd ever done. Also, *The Miseducation of Lauryn Hill* had come out a few years before and I listened to that record over and over. I wanted *World Without Tears* to have some qualities that she put together, hip-hop and spoken word stuff.

With the songs in hand, I went into the studio with my band, Doug Pettibone on guitars, Taras Prodaniuk on bass, and Jim Christie on drums. Doug and Jim both grew up right on the coast, somewhere near Oxnard or Ventura, and were dedicated surfers. Taras had grown up in the Valley. These guys were L.A. boys through and through and they could play almost any kind of music.

When we started considering producers for the record, I was still thinking in the mode of Dylan's *Time Out of Mind* sound. An engineer named Mark Howard had worked with

Daniel Lanois to produce that record and he also worked with Lanois on Emmylou's *Wrecking Ball* and many others. A lot of the records that Mark made with Lanois were recorded in old houses in New Orleans that had been turned into studios. Mark had recently done the same thing in Silver Lake, built a studio in an old house, so we sought him out and he agreed to work with us.

Mark's new studio was in an eighteen-thousand-square-foot mansion on a hilltop. It was built in the 1920s by a socialite woman who had inherited a bunch of oil money. She was married to a silent-film actor and apparently they had massive parties there with guests like Buster Keaton and Charlie Chaplin. The architecture was Spanish Mediterranean and it was built by the same guy who built Beverly Hills High School and some other famous places. There were twenty-foot ceilings and massive windows. The grounds spread out over five acres and had three cottages for staff. Once there was a citrus orchard and a horse farm on the property.

The original owners died young and the mansion was turned into a boarding school for orphan girls during the Great Depression. Then, in the 1950s, the estate gave the spread to the Immaculate Conception Home for Girls, which was run by Catholic nuns from Mexico, and that's what it was until the 1990s.

In the late 1990s the sisters tried to sell the estate and couldn't find any buyers because the property was so immense and was in such a state of disrepair and the immedi-

218

ate neighborhood around it had a reputation for crime and vice.

Which means, of course, it was the perfect place for a kick-ass recording studio, which is exactly what Mark Howard built there.

Today it's a boutique hotel called the Paramour. Back when we were recording there, it was rumored to be haunted and I wouldn't doubt it. The spirits of orphan girls occupied that place for seventy years. Doug Pettibone stayed there while we were recording and he said he could hear voices and other strange sounds all the time. He loved it.

When the record came out, there was a great review written by Ann Powers that described the situation pretty well in her opening lines:

On first listen, Lucinda Williams' new record inspires one overriding thought: *This chick is crazy.* Here she is, 50 years old, America's most respected songwriter—and she puts out a disc full of snarls, mumbles and groans that fixate on one failed, possibly sleazy romance, songs veering from spiritual lunacy to gutter-level misery. The rock numbers are nasty and the ballads bloody, and she makes two attempts at, yes, rap. This is not how elders are supposed to behave.

Exactly. I don't clip many reviews, don't even read many of them, but somebody pointed this one out to me and I put it in my scrapbook.

Looking back, I can see that *Car Wheels, Essence,* and *World Without Tears* form some sort of trilogy, although I didn't envision it that way. My career had been about taking small steps over a long period of time and in those three records, which came out in a five-year span, everything was uncorked. We recorded *World Without Tears* in a way similar to how we recorded the Rough Trade record. We went into the Paramour and we just cranked the songs out. We wanted it live and fresh and gnarly. The trilogy, in a way, is like three different ways of making music about sex, love, and the state of the world—or my world.

22

I was fifty-one years old and my life and work had never been hotter. I was either on the road with my band or living at the Safari Inn.

On March 8, 2004, we were playing a sold-out show in Charlotte, North Carolina. We were backstage and the theater was rocking. As we were about to go onstage, a phone call came in to the theater's offices. I can't remember who called me. My mother had passed away. To say I was devastated doesn't say enough. Every emotion imaginable came rushing to the surface at once. There was no way I would be able to play that show, so we had to cancel it literally right at curtains. The presenter went out onstage and told the audience what had happened and I was later told that the audience took the news rather well. There were no boos or anything like that. We had to cancel a number of other shows, too.

She was seventy-three years old, and even though she'd been struggling with lung issues, her death was sudden. She had continued to live in New Orleans until I helped her get into an assisted living facility in Fayetteville, which I'd paid for.

She had remarried to a good man many years before, an exploration geologist. He'd passed away before she did, and she didn't have a will. So as the oldest child the legal power of attorney went to me.

The tour bus drove us from Charlotte to Fayetteville, almost a thousand miles, something like a fourteen-hour drive. We left directly from the theater that night. Of course my father and stepmother were living in Fayetteville, and by the time I arrived, my stepmother was trying to plan a funeral and memorial for my mother. Once I arrived, they stepped into the background and were very supportive.

However, my mother's brother Cecil arrived and what ensued was an absolute nightmare for me, one of the worst experiences of my life. My mother didn't want to have a lot of money spent on her funeral. She told me she didn't want a casket and all that. She wanted to be cremated and her remains put in an urn.

When Uncle Cecil heard the news of my mother's death, he and his wife drove from their home in Sulphur, Louisiana, to Fayetteville. I was at the funeral parlor picking out an urn when they walked in. Uncle Cecil insisted that there be a casket and a traditional funeral and that my mother be buried in Monroe, Louisiana, beside her parents. That's the fucking last thing my mother would have wanted.

The situation was impossible. I was overwhelmed with so much emotion and felt I was manipulated into agreeing to a regular funeral. The whole thing ended up costing eleven thousand dollars, which I agreed to pay for. My brother and sister arrived and the chaos just kept mounting and I couldn't see through it. I was too emotional. I ended up picking out the casket and then the vault that the casket sits in. Then the funeral parlor director asked me, "What about some of these angels?" and he showed me these little ceramic angels that would be placed on each corner of the casket. He told me my brother, sister, and I could take replicas of those angels home as souvenirs. And on and on it went like that.

With my sister, Karyn.

So much of Mom's therapy was about coming to terms with the damage her parents and family did to her, damage she struggled with her entire life. The fact that they were driving her body to Monroe to be laid beside her parents was too much for me. I couldn't go to the burial.

I eventually dealt with this pain by writing a song about it. "Fancy Funeral" came out on my 2007 record, *West*.

> Some think a fancy funeral
> Would be worth every cent
> For every dime and nickel
> There's money better spent
>
> Better spent on groceries
> And covering the bills
> Instead of little luxuries
> And unnecessary frills
>
> Lovely yellow daffodils
> And lacy filigree
> Pretty little angels
> For everyone to see
>
> Lily of the valley
> Long black limousines
> It's three or four months' salary
> Just to pay for all those things
>
> So don't buy a fancy funeral
> It's not worth it in the end

Goodbyes can still be beautiful
With all the money that you'll spend

'Cause no amount of riches
Can bring back what you've lost
To satisfy your wishes
You'll never justify the cost

Still today, knowing my mother is buried where she did not want to be is deeply hurtful to me.

My relationship with my family has been something that I've spent many hours in therapy trying to process. My mother, toward the end of her days, asked me to forgive her. And I did. I never openly discussed with her what I'd learned about the sexual abuse she'd endured when she was a kid. But knowing about it helped me understand how challenging her emotional and psychological life had been.

My father was my anchor because my mother was mentally ill. But he had his problems, too. My family wasn't allowed to talk about problems out loud. Everything was held inside. I was never able to tell anybody that I was upset or pissed off. Looking back, I wonder if it would have been better if you could yell and scream and say, "Fuck you!" and slam the door and leave. Then the next day it's all over with, and you start again.

My therapist refers to "frozen moments," when a traumatic event or traumatic experience is frozen in your psyche and it can cause physical ailments, from acid reflux to migraine headaches to whatever else. One of those frozen moments for me, she says, is when my mother locked me in the closet when I was three years old because she couldn't deal with normal things that a three-year-old does. She told me to take this psychic traumatic moment and visualize it like a physical thing and actually go into that closet and talk to the little girl and comfort her and bring her out of the closet and hold her in my arms. My therapist led me through the exercise. She had me close my eyes and just bring the little girl out of the closet and tell her she's safe and everything is okay and she's going to be safe. She kept saying, "Keep holding her until you feel like she becomes one with you." In other words, the little three-year-old girl and the sixty-eight-year-old woman are not separate. We're the same person. You have to go in and take hold of the little child and hold her and tell her things are going to be okay, it's going to be okay, it's going to be okay. And then I became one with the little girl and I felt so much better. It was a guided visualization state and I told my therapist I didn't want my three-year-old self to disappear and she said, "She won't disappear. She's going to join you and you are going to make her safe and okay." It's about love. You love that part of yourself, the three-year-old you. You love her and you embrace her and she exists in you. You love her as much as you can, you give her everything you have.

Looking back at my life, I can see clearly this tendency I had to find these rough-and-tumble men who suffered from a lot of emotional problems but who could also be very sweet and quite intelligent, more intelligent and interesting than most. Many of these men had suffered from some sort of abuse in their childhoods, so they were left with adult struggles that some might call PTSD today. They were emotionally unpredictable. They had Jekyll-and-Hyde-type personalities.

I can also see that my mother suffered from this emotional disorder, too. It had to be caused by the severe sexual abuse inflicted by her father and her older brothers. As I get older, my mother's story makes me madder and madder. Her father hid behind the church pulpit. He hid behind the Bible. He hid behind the cross. To think of him standing up there preaching to a congregation, it's horrifying and disgusting. He should have been put in jail. To think that I sat in his lap when I was a kid makes my stomach turn. My grandpa, somebody who was supposed to protect me and love me. He ruined my mother's life. She never had a chance.

For my 2003 album, *World Without Tears,* I wrote a song about this kind of haunting emotional struggle that people have after they've been abused as kids. I had one particular former boyfriend in mind when I wrote this song. He was somebody I met when I was living in Nashville. He was a bartender and sometimes a bass player. But he really could have been anybody. The song could be about anyone. It's called "Sweet Side."

You run yourself ragged tryin' to be strong
You feel bad when you done nothin' wrong
Love got all confused with anger and pride
So much abuse on such a little child

Someone you trusted told you to shut up
Now there's a pain in your gut that you can't get
    rid of
No one heard your screams when you were nine
When bad dreams filled your summertime

So you don't always show your sweet side
You don't always show your sweet side . . .

You're tough as steel and you keep your chin up
You don't ever feel like you're good enough
You've had the blues ever since you were six
Your little tennis shoes and your pick-up sticks

You were screamed at and kicked over and over
Now you always feel sick and you can't keep a
    lover
Every Christmas there were presents to unwrap
But the things you witnessed when you were
    five and a half

So you don't always show your sweet side
You don't always show your sweet side . . .

Someone deserted you, the damage is done
Now you don't deserve to be loved by no one

Don't Tell Anybody the Secrets I Told You

Hands that would feed you when you were two
Were the same hands that beat you black and
    blue

You get defensive at every turn
You're overly sensitive and overly concerned
Few precious memories, no lullabies
Hollowed out centuries of lies

You don't always show your sweet side
You don't always show your sweet side . . .

I've seen you in the kitchen cookin' me
    supper
I listened to you bitchin' and I watched you
    suffer
I still love you baby 'cause I know you
Don't mean to do the cruel things you do

I've seen you sewin' buttons on your shirt
I've seen you throwin' up when your stomach
    hurt
I stick by you baby through thick and thin
No matter what kind of shape you're in

'Cause I've seen your sweet side
I've seen your sweet side

I've seen your sweet side, baby
I've seen your sweet side

This tendency of mine reached a violent low point, a nadir, in 2004 when I was back living in Los Angeles. It was around the time my mother passed away. My career was soaring, so you'd think that I would have grown out of this pattern—a huge range of people were interested in me, including relatively stable people—but those patterns are hard to break.

I had a show at a winery in California, a beautiful spot somewhere along the coast. I noticed this member of the crew staff who was good-looking and gentle. He was like a puppy dog—Mama, can I take him home?

His name was Matthew Greeson. At the time he was living in a sober-living house in Los Angeles. He'd been there for some time and he'd improved to the point where he could take jobs outside the treatment center. He looked very healthy and happy to me. I thought, "He's sober. He's safe. He's been through a serious program and he's straightened up. He's matured and because of his program he's got a leg up on all the other troubled men I've been with."

I thought I didn't have to worry about him, that he'd taken the steps most people never take to get into a program and straighten himself out. What I didn't realize clearly enough is that there was a reason he was in that treatment center to begin with. He wasn't ready to get out into the world yet.

I had been around a lot of people—men and women—who drank a lot, who partied hard, but almost all of them were just looking to relax and have a good time. The more they drank, the more they laughed. They were drinking to have fun. Celebrant, jovial types for the most part. They were looking to forget their problems for a few hours, not to cause more problems for themselves or anyone else.

Matthew was a different sort. After we were together a while, he started imbibing here and there. He said he had it under control and I believed him, or I wanted to believe him. He was real sweet to me at first and I loved him for that. Pretty soon, though, he started drinking more and he would get hostile over nothing. The littlest thing would set him off and he'd get steaming angry. It was almost like he'd black out while still being conscious. The next day he wouldn't remember what he'd said or done. The next day he'd also have the puppy dog thing going again. He'd be real sweet. "I'm sorry . . . I'm sorry."

Like with so many of these guys I fell for, I thought I could help him get it together. I would encourage him to continue his therapy in an outpatient manner. I'd support him through that. I didn't know that these hostile spirals would ascend to a totally awful level.

One night Matthew and I were in Memphis staying at the famous Peabody hotel. It is a grand downtown hotel that has been there since the early twentieth century. There is a huge lobby with a fountain in the middle, and for decades mallard ducks have been living in the hotel. They swim in the fountain and walk around the hotel.

I can't remember why we were in Memphis, but I remember being exhausted and wanting to go to sleep. Matthew said he was going to go to the bar downstairs and have a drink. So he did. When he came back to the room, he was a totally different person. He was angry and hostile for no apparent reason. I wanted to go to sleep, but he had other things that he wanted to do to me. He wanted to have rough sex with me or something. I went into this mode I can go into to protect myself—a complacent mode, to appease him and calm him down. I let him take my clothes off. We were both naked. We started wrestling. At first it was playful and then he started to get more and more aggressive. He pushed me down on the bed and held me down, choking me with his arm over my chest. He got rougher and rougher. I couldn't move. I began to get scared. It was the first time I had been this scared with him. I thought he actually might kill me. I thought I might actually die in the Peabody hotel.

I somehow found the energy to squirm free from him. My fight-flight responses were kicking in hard. I was fighting to survive. All I could think of was getting on the phone and calling the front desk. I went over and grabbed the phone. He jumped on me and tore the phone out of my hands. I ran to the door and somehow made it out into the hallway. I was still buck naked. Matthew came raging out into the hallway, naked as well, and the door closed behind him and we were locked out without a key. I was now thinking that somebody was going to recognize me and this was going to end up in a magazine. I could see the headline: "Lucinda Williams Was Found Naked in a Hallway in the Peabody Hotel." I thought, "Oh my God, my fans are going to know about this."

I scrunched down into a ball on the floor. I was in a sitting fetal position with my head between my knees. Matthew, for some reason, lay down spread eagle on the hallway floor. Soon, a hotel security staffer showed up. He opened our door and let us back into our room. Then he walked away. Back in our room, we both took a temporary sigh of relief. That episode was over. I was ignorant enough to think it wouldn't happen again.

We made it back to Los Angeles, to my apartment in Burbank. Matthew told me that he was doing heroin but he had it under control, which was obviously not the case. I told him he needed to get more treatment, that he needed professional medical help. I don't know why I stayed with him. I never actually saw him taking those drugs. It turns out he was doing speedballs—mixing heroin and cocaine—in the basement of my apartment building near the laundry room. I had never been with anyone, intimately, who had done drugs like that.

By this time I had amassed a fairly impressive collection of folk art, what some people call outsider art, by Howard Finster and artists like that. At some point I began to notice that a piece or two was missing, but I never said anything. I don't know what I was thinking. Then I noticed that one of my Grammys was missing. I suspected that Matthew was stealing these things and hocking them for money to buy his drugs. When I approached Matthew about this, he flew into a violent rage. The rest of the story is told in my song "Wakin' Up" on my 2020 album, *Good Souls Better Angels*.

Doin' speedballs on the basement
Still all my mind, I can't erase it
That demon I hear, he had to chase it
I says he's clean, he's tryin' embrace it
But he's a bad man, he has to face it
'Til all my mind, I can erase it

But I'm waking up from a bad dream
I'm shaking up, it was a bad scene
But I'm waking up from a bad dream
It shook me up, it was a bad scene
But I'm waking up, it shook me up
But I'm waking up, it fucked me up
But I'm waking up from a bad dream

Yeah, he threw a punch, somehow, I missed it
I should've split, thought I could fix it
He pulled the kitchen chair out from under me
He pulled my hair and then he pissed on me
Next thing, I swear, he wants a kiss on me
After all this, he wants a kiss on me

But I'm waking up from a bad dream

Before the album was released, I played the song for an artist whose opinion I respect. He said, "Lu, I don't know if you want to put this song out in the world. Everyone is going to ask you questions about what happened."

I did it anyway. I wanted to tell my story. I thought it might help women in similar situations.

After that night, I called a friend. She brought me a copy of the AA manual, thinking that would give me some ideas of what I should do. Eventually, I took Matthew back to rehab. He knew he needed to go.

I moved out of my apartment and back into the Safari Inn by myself. The Safari Inn was always my happy place, where I felt the safest and most comfortable.

23

I wrote most of the songs that appeared on my next two albums, *West* (2007) and *Little Honey* (2008), at the Safari Inn. Many of those songs, especially on *West*, are in one way or another about me working through my emotions after my mother's passing. Another way I got through it was by playing as many shows as possible with Doug, Jim, and Taras, and we released a live album, *Live at the Fillmore*, in 2005.

With the success of *World Without Tears* and the increasing opportunities for me, Luke Lewis at Lost Highway gave me a budget of half a million dollars for my next record. I bought some time at Radio Recorders studio in Hollywood, where Frank Sinatra had made many of his records, and I made demos of twenty-four songs that I'd written at the Safari Inn.

I also met my husband in 2005. One night I was at the infamous Whisky a Go Go in Hollywood to see Hank Williams III, the grandson of Hank Williams, who was fusing punk and country in a unique way. I was standing in the audience when a guy named Damien approached me with an offer to cut my hair and handed me his business card. A few days later I took him up on the offer and threw in an appointment for a close friend of mine, Shilah Morrow, as a birthday gift. Located in Hollywood near Sunset and Vine, the salon was appropriately named Hairroin. I went first and Damien had started in on Shilah's hair when he excused himself for a second to meet his last appointment of the day, who was just coming in the door. I looked up and took notice of a tall and slim man with a broad smile and flashing blue eyes. His smile revealed a shiny silver tooth, which I loved. Damien introduced us. His name was Tom Overby, and he told me that we had a mutual friend, Bonnie Butler from Minneapolis. He had recently moved to Los Angeles from Minneapolis, where he had been the music buyer for Best Buy. He had gotten a record label job in L.A. at Fontana, which was part of Universal.

Shilah and I had made plans for later that night to see a friend of ours, Susan Mitchell, sing a block away at the Hotel Cafe, but we had a little time before that started, so we were going to go up the street to the Velvet Margarita for a drink.

Tom came with us and we drank a little tequila—the Velvet Margarita is a favorite Hollywood Mexican place with decor that includes velvet Elvises and Day of the Dead folk art. After a couple of tequilas and tortilla chips, we headed to the Hotel Cafe. A while later, I was starting to feel the tequila and I knew I shouldn't drive home, so Tom offered to drive me home to the Safari Inn. I was smitten.

One night soon after we met, I invited Tom to come over to Radio Recorders to listen to my new songs after he left his office at Universal. Even before we met, Tom had carefully listened to all my records. He's carefully listened to all of everybody's records. That's what he does. We got a bottle of good wine and we sat and listened to all of the songs. Tom said, "I'm sincerely blown away. This is another advance in your music. If you release these all on one record, it's going to be your *Exile on Main St.*"

A short time after that Tom asked me if I wanted to go to the Bruce Springsteen show at the Pantages Theatre in Hollywood. It was the Devils & Dust Tour and Springsteen was playing smaller theaters by himself, without his band. Tom said he could get tickets, but I said, hold on, let me make a call, and I called Frank Callari. Soon enough we had tickets and backstage passes.

Bruce's show was incredible and we went backstage afterward. It was quite a scene. Jim Carrey came up to meet me and was raving about my music. We met Sam Moore of the legendary Sam & Dave. There were some people I knew back there like T-Bone Burnett and his wife, Callie, and my old friend Jesse Malin, who was the singer in the great New York punk band D Generation. When Bruce came over to me and said, "Hey, Lu, how ya doin'?" I was kind of overwhelmed and had trouble getting the words out, but I guess I managed to say something decent, because a few minutes later, after the crowd thinned out, Bruce came over to me and Tom and invited us to dinner. We went to Kate Mantilini's well-known West Hollywood restaurant. It was Bruce, T-Bone and Callie, Jesse, the Edge from U2 and his wife, and me and Tom, a man I'd known for only a couple of weeks. It was exciting but also sort of stunning and otherworldly. Bruce kept trying to strike up a conversation with me and I struggled at first, but I eventually got there. Going through my head all night were questions like do you call the Edge "the Edge" in person or just "Edge," or does he have a street name? What does his wife call him? The fact is that they were lovely people and I shouldn't have been so nervous.

Eventually, Bruce got up and said he had to leave but everybody was welcome to stay and the bill was covered. When he walked up to me and Tom to say goodbye, Tom told Bruce, "I saw an interview with you several years ago where you said that rock and roll reached down into your house and pulled you out, and I just want to tell you that you did that for me. I wouldn't be sitting here right now if it weren't for you."

Bruce leaned over and gave Tom a big bear hug and he said, "Thanks, man, that really means a lot."

On the drive back home, I said to Tom, "That was really sweet, what you said to Bruce and the way you said it." He was still a man I barely knew, but I was starting to have a feeling that he'd be around for a while.

For our third date, we went to see Jason Molina and his band Magnolia Electric Co. at a dive in Echo Park. Tom introduced me to Molina's music and then I became enamored with his records. I'd like to cover some of his songs one day. I remember Tom and me talking about record sales or personal finances that night, and he said, "I'm good with numbers," and I thought that was so hot. He also had just the right amount of bling. I'd never been around a man like that before.

On our first "date," we listened to my new songs at Radio Recorders. Our second date was the night with Bruce and friends. Then the Jason Molina concert. Not a bad start to what became a successful and lasting marriage.

Tom became a formidable new presence in my life. He wasn't one of these down-and-out poet-motorcycle-bad-boy guys who could barely hold it together. He was wicked smart. He's also got this ability to know that whenever I'm in a bad mood, it's just a mood, it's not a problem or something that needs to be discussed or challenged or escaped from. He rolls with it. One night a few years after I met Tom, tensions were sky-high during a recording session at Village Record-ers on Santa Monica Boulevard. I had a meltdown and ran out of the studio and disappeared. I walked all over the neighborhood. I had done this kind of thing before. Tom came out and walked the streets trying to find me. He was calling my cell and texting but I wasn't responding. I had circled several blocks many times and Tom was still calling me and texting me. He told me he was scared. It wasn't a ter-rible neighborhood for a woman to be walking late at night, but it wasn't a great one, either.

Finally I answered.

"What?"

"What do you mean, 'What'? Where are you?"

"Over here."

"Over where?"

"Behind you."

Tom turned around and looked and I was standing kitty-corner across the intersection from the studio, under a streetlight in front of Floyd's Barbershop. I knew then that he'd always be by my side.

24

A few years after I started dating Tom, an article appeared in *Rolling Stone* in which I mentioned I was going out with him. At the time Tom was working at Universal, and he said that after some of his colleagues read the *Rolling Stone* article, they went up to him and said something to the effect of "Be careful, our reps at her label tell us that she's literally insane." Tom was smart enough to know that there are many male artists who make creative decisions the way I do and nobody calls them insane. He knows women have been treated differently for millennia.

I knew I wanted to marry Tom. He was so smart and so kind, unlike anybody else I'd ever been with. It's something you feel. You just know, this is it.

In 2006, Tom was with me on the tour bus. We were living in Los Angeles and the bus was in Nashville. It was a relatively short tour, just me and Doug Pettibone on guitars and my father reading a few poems.

On the bus Tom said to me, "You want to go shopping for diamonds?" That's how he proposed. Tom says that I'm the one who said that, not him. He says that I said, "When are you gonna get me a diamond?" That's not how I remember it. We laugh about it today.

The next show after Nashville was two days later in Minneapolis. Tom said he knew a great jewelry store in Omaha, which was right on the way to Minneapolis. We took the bus to Omaha and stayed overnight in the parking lot next to the jewelry store so we'd have plenty of time to make a decision when the store opened the next day.

Trouble is, my OCD kicked in that morning when I knew I was going to have to make a decision on the ring. I wanted to make the decision because I loved Tom so much, but I was also feeling overwhelmed. I was so nervous. I struggled to get dressed to go into the store. It took hours. I was a nervous wreck. It was far more nerve-racking than playing a show. I would have done anything to take my mind off picking a ring. I told Tom, "You're getting a good look at my neurotic side."

"I've seen it many times before," he said.

"Do you still want to marry me?" I asked.

"Yes, I do," he said.

Finally, twenty minutes before the store closed, we went inside. There were so many options. I knew I didn't want a ring with a big, fat diamond sticking up. I wanted one with diamonds set inside the band. There was a "don't touch anything" vibe in the store. I felt like everybody was looking at me. "Make a decision, lady, make a decision."

I made a decision. We were officially engaged. We got on the bus and drove to the next tour stop in Minneapolis.

My husband, Tom, and me.

Not long after that Tom said to me, "Let's get married onstage," and I thought that was a great idea. Then we decided we wanted to do it at First Avenue, the famous club in Minneapolis where I had played many times. Tom is from there and it felt like a good place to do it. The clincher was, when I told my father our plan, he said, "That's perfect. Hank Williams got married onstage."

It took a couple of years to fit First Avenue into our tour schedule. We eventually married on September 18, 2009:

9-18-9. It forms one of my life-path numbers in numerology terms. I can be a little bit New Agey, which is something that dates back to my years working in health food stores. Nine is the month. One and eight make nine. And the year was nine.

It turned out to be a gorgeous day. We all stayed in a hotel across the street from First Avenue. We rented out a restaurant on the next block. Everything was within walking distance. It was a big party.

We'd invited around half the audience that was there—our friends who had flown into town for the show and wedding. The other half didn't know they'd witness a wedding. I think some of my fans might have heard rumors about it.

The band played a normal set and we performed the wedding to start the encore. My father officiated the ceremony and he read his poem "The Caterpillar," which is about me.

> Today on the lip of a bowl in the backyard we
> > watched a caterpillar caught in the circle of
> > his larval assumptions
> my daughter counted
> 27 times he went around
> before rolling back and laughing
> I'm a caterpillar, look
> she left him
> measuring out his slow green way to some place
> > there must have been a picture of inside him
> After supper
> coming from putting the car up

we stopped to look
figured he crossed the yard
once every hour
and left him
when we went to bed
wrinkling no closer to my landlord's leaves
than when he somehow fell into his private circle
Later I followed
barefeet and doorclicks of my daughter
to the yard the bowl
a milkwhite moonlight eye
in the black grass
it died
I said honey they don't live very long
In bed again
re-covered and re-kissed
she locked her arms and mumbling love to mine
   until yawning she slipped
into the deep bone-bottomed dish of sleep
Stumbling drunk around the rim
I hold
the words she said to me across the dark
I think he thought he was
going in a straight line.

My father also wrote our wedding vows, which contained a lot of humor, including this line: "I love you for all the things I do not, yet, know."

After the ceremony we played "Happy" by the Rolling Stones. Tom grabbed a guitar and played along with us.

After our wedding we jumped back on the bus and continued the tour. We didn't have a honeymoon. Our honeymoon was on the tour bus, which is a place where we still today feel quite at home together.

Tom and I bought a house in Studio City a year and a half before our wedding. We still have that house today, although we split our time between Los Angeles and Nashville.

Sometime in 2010 my stepmother, Jordan, wrote me a letter explaining that my father had been diagnosed with Alzheimer's disease. She was beside herself. I remember she told me that she didn't even know if she was spelling the word correctly. In the package with the letter she included a book about Alzheimer's called *Still Alice*. It's a novel by Lisa Genova about a woman, Alice, who has an early-onset version of the disease. The message of the novel is that the woman who was Alice is still there, still in that body, even though parts of her seem to be lost as each day passes. But she's still in there, the same Alice.

Tom and I went to visit my father and stepmother in Fayetteville for the Christmas holidays later that year. We were in the sunroom off the living room of the house alone with my father. Jordan must have been upstairs asleep. We'd had one of our normal evenings of drinking wine and talking and listening to music. My father was still able to hold it together when we were present. But that night he told us something that hit me like a ton of bricks. He told us that his disease had progressed to the point that he could no longer write poetry and read his work aloud in public. To me, it was the saddest thing he could say. "Honey, I can't write anymore." It was like saying he couldn't see or couldn't talk anymore.

Such a central part of him had died. That's the way that disease works. Things fade away or break off and crumble and die gradually. It was unbearable to see that part of him disappear. The disease had chipped away a part of him that was his identity.

That night I got a yellow legal pad and wrote him a long note that I left on the kitchen table for him to read in the morning. I told him that even though he could no longer write poetry, he was still a poet.

The next morning he told me the note moved him. He hugged me and thanked me. He also told me the note was beautifully written. Always the teacher.

Over the next four years my father would slowly lose the rest of himself. In late 2014 he was moved into a memory care unit of assisted living and he passed away on January 1, 2015.

It was not lost on me that Hank Williams had passed away on New Year's Day, too. Nineteen fifty-three, the month and year I was born.

Too cool to be forgotten.

EPILOGUE

A few years after we got married, Tom became my manager, and as I said in the liner notes to my album *West*,
he changed my life for the better. *West* came out on February
13, 2007, and three weeks later I was scheduled to play the
biggest show of my career. I had sold out Radio City Music
Hall in New York City in two days after tickets went on sale.
I'd played many huge festivals, but this was the biggest venue
that I had ever sold out as a headliner, around six thousand
seats. It was also the biggest show of any artist on Lost
Highway Records, so many of the executives were flying in
for the show. It was a high-water mark for all involved. A
couple of nights before the show Tom and I were sitting
outside in front of the bar next to our hotel and I suddenly

realized that the street corner half a block away, the corner at Fifty-fourth Street and Seventh Avenue, had been an important place in my life.

I looked at Tom and said, "This is so unbelievably strange."

"What?"

"You're not going to believe this, but that corner is one of the corners I used to play for change at when I briefly lived here back in '79. I lived in Brooklyn long before everybody lived in Brooklyn. Several times a week I would take the subway to this corner and play for tips to be thrown into my guitar case."

"Are you kidding me?"

"Nope," I said. "That's the spot. It feels like a dream now."

POSTSCRIPT

As I was writing some of the final pages of this book in the middle of 2022, I felt like I had something else to say. I pulled out a yellow legal pad and wrote these thoughts on living a good life, just from my point of view:

> Read. You should read Bukowski and Ferlinghetti, read Sylvia Plath and Anne Sexton, and listen to Coltrane, Nina Simone, Hank Williams, Loretta Lynn, Son House, Robert Johnson, Howlin' Wolf, Lightnin' Hopkins, Miles Davis, Lou Reed, Nick Drake, Bobbie Gentry, George Jones, Jimmy Reed, Odetta, Funkadelic, and Woody Guthrie.

Drive across America. Ride trains. Fly to countries beyond your comfort zone. Try different things. Join hands across the water. Different foods. New tasks. Different menus and tastes.

Talk with the guy who's working in construction on your block, who's working on the highway you're traveling on. Speak with your neighbors. Get to know them. Practice civil disobedience. Try new resistance. Be part of the solution, not the problem.

Don't litter the earth, it's the only one you have, learn to love her. Care for her. Learn another language. Trust your friends with kindness. You will need them one day. You will need earth one day. Do not fear death. There are worse things than death. Do not fear the reaper.

Lie in the sunshine but from time to time let the neon light your way. ZZ Top, Jefferson Airplane, Spirit. Get a haircut. Dye your hair pink or blue. Do it for you. Wear eyeliner. Your eyes are the windows to your soul. Show them off. Wear a feather in your cap. Run around like the Mad Hatter. Perhaps he had the answer.

Visit the desert. Go to the zoo. Go to a county fair. Ride the Ferris wheel. Ride a horse. Pet a pig. Ride a donkey. Protest against war. Put a peace symbol on your automobile. Drive a Volkswagen. Slow down for skateboarders. They might have the answers. Eat gingerbread men. Pray to the moon and the stars. God is out there somewhere. Don't worry. You'll find out where soon enough.

Postscript

Dance. Even if you don't know how to dance. Read *The Four Agreements*. Read the Bible. Read the Bhagavad Gita. Join nothing. It won't help. No games, no church, no religion, no yellow-brick road, no way to Oz. Wear beads. Watch a caterpillar in the sun.

Acknowledgments

This book has been in the making my whole life, but in a literal sense, six years.

First and foremost, thank you to my sister Karyn and brother Robert for riding with me down all those gravel roads.

Next, much gratitude to my editor, Gillian Blake, for her patience, trust, understanding, and guiding light. This simply couldn't have happened without her.

To David McCormick at McCormick Literary Agency for believing in my story from the very beginning.

To Nicky Dawidoff for bringing David into my universe and also for early support and advice.

To Sam Stephenson for doing all the dirty work and pulling all the parts together to mold this book into this wonderful final shape.

Back around 2010, Sam read an interview with me talking about concert film footage of my shows that we've stockpiled. He got my email address from Joe Henry and wrote me a letter offering to help me figure out what to do with that footage. My husband, Tom Overby, responded and kept in touch with him. Then in 2019 we brought Sam into the book project. He's from a small town in eastern North Carolina and his mother was from Galax, Virginia, so he could relate to a lot of my background. He started with about a hundred hours of interviews that Tom had done with me. Then he did his own hundred hours of interviews with me in Nashville. After a while I said, "I don't need a therapist when I have Sam." I wrote memories and stories on legal pads, a couple hundred single-spaced pages. From all this, we crafted chapters and passages that Sam and I went over at our kitchen table line by line over a couple of years. Sam's friend the writer Darcey Steinke read the manuscript at several points and offered feedback. And, of course, enormous thanks to Gillian's staff at Crown for their input and support all along.

I also owe lifelong thanks to many important people in my life for weighing in on certain aspects of this story: David Clements, Cranston Clements, John Biguenet, Bill Priest, Ralph Adamo, Hobart Taylor, David Hirschland, Brian Cullman, David Miner, David Mansfield, Greg Sowders, Bill

Bentley, Rosemary Carroll, Frank Riley, Dusty Wakeman, Steve Earle, Ray Kennedy, Robin Hurley, Luke Lewis, Peggy French, and Don Todd.

In addition, I thank my colleagues Travis Stephens and John Stone. There's not much that I do, at home or on the road, without them. And many thanks to Jim Flammia for everything he does for us.

Finally, and ultimately, I can't say enough about my husband, Tom, who has been with me, and me with him, for eighteen years. His love is what I was trying to find. The existence of this book, and much more, owes so much to him.

LW

January 2023

Permissions

About the Author

LUCINDA WILLIAMS is an iconic rock, folk, and country music singer, songwriter, and musician. A seventeen-time Grammy Award nominee and three-time winner, she has also been nominated twelve times for the Americana Award, which she has won twice. Williams was named "America's best songwriter" by *Time* and one of the "100 Greatest Songwriters of All Time" by *Rolling Stone.*